S0-BDM-834

A SCOOP OF
HELL
BETWEEN TWO
SLICES OF
HEAVEN

MAGGIE SUMMERS

ARCHWAY
PUBLISHING

Copyright © 2017 Maggie Summers.

All rights reserved. No part of this book may be used or reproduced by any means, graphic, electronic, or mechanical, including photocopying, recording, taping or by any information storage retrieval system without the written permission of the author except in the case of brief quotations embodied in critical articles and reviews.

Scripture quotations marked NIV are taken from the Holy Bible, New International Version. NIV. Copyright 1973, 1978, 1984 by International Bible Society. Used by permission of Zondervan. All rights reserved.

This book is a work of non-fiction. Unless otherwise noted, the author and the publisher make no explicit guarantees as to the accuracy of the information contained in this book and in some cases, names of people and places have been altered to protect their privacy.

Archway Publishing books may be ordered through booksellers or by contacting:

Archway Publishing
1663 Liberty Drive
Bloomington, IN 47403
www.archwaypublishing.com
1 (888) 242-5904

Because of the dynamic nature of the Internet, any web addresses or links contained in this book may have changed since publication and may no longer be valid. The views expressed in this work are solely those of the author and do not necessarily reflect the views of the publisher, and the publisher hereby disclaims any responsibility for them.

Any people depicted in stock imagery provided by Thinkstock are models, and such images are being used for illustrative purposes only. Certain stock imagery © Thinkstock.

ISBN: 978-1-4808-4801-6 (sc)
ISBN: 978-1-4808-4802-3 (e)

Library of Congress Control Number: 2017908373

Print information available on the last page.

Archway Publishing rev. date: 06/08/2017

This book is dedicated to my dear husband, my knight in shining armor, who taught me how to love. I love him more today than I did yesterday, and I will love him more tomorrow than I love him today.

CONTENTS

PROLOGUE

Have you always been perfect? A friend asked me that question not long ago. I humorously replied, "No. Today is my first day." I pondered that exchange many times. Why would she ask me that question? I've never thought I was perfect, especially not during my forty-year marriage. Quite the opposite. My husband never failed to tell me how imperfect I was. In fact, he would introduce me as his semi-beautiful wife. In private, he called me a jerk and an asshole—nowhere near honey or sweetheart. He blamed me for everything from the war in Vietnam to his hangnail. I was especially responsible for his need for alcohol. Oh, if only I would change, he could stop drinking. After much reflection, I saw there was truth in my friend's comment. I do find a need to be perfect, because I was told how imperfect I was.

I'm writing my story for two reasons. First, I believe that God has been a motivating force in my life. I have God's message of saving grace to share with others. Through my challenges in life the Lord has opened my heart to the needs of suffering people. The Holy Spirit has gifted me with compassion and love for others. Second, I want you to know you are not alone when dealing with domestic violence. From my experiences, I hope you may learn the signs that say you're not being treated with respect, and then seek help.

PART I

A FIRST SLICE OF HEAVEN

CHAPTER 1

Born with a Silver Spoon in My Mouth

Learning about our ancestors tells us where we came from, who we are, and where we are going. What I know about my past begins with my paternal grandparents, Lawrence and Olivia. They had two children, Ruth, born in 1901, and Karl, born in 1903. The family lived on a prosperous farm in Medina, Ohio, where the cornfields ran for miles and miles. The property bordered on a major highway, making it very attractive. Kmart bought the land and built one of its first stores there. The family's newfound wealth may have been the reason Grandma carried her black leather purse with her everywhere she went and hung on to the straps. I saw her open it on Sundays to put an offering in the collection plate and on special occasions like when my Dad wanted a Chris-Craft cabin cruiser to speed around the Great Lakes.

Lawrence died of a stroke when I was small and impressionable. I remember watching all of Grandpa's clothes being put in a pile in a cornfield and set on fire. It made me very sad. I guess there were no Goodwill or Salvation Army stores back then.

My dad, Karl, never graduated from high school, something quite common in the 1920s. He met my mother, Helen, from Litchfield, Ohio, while she was attending Medina Community College. But if it was unusual to graduate from high school back then, how did Helen have the opportunity to obtain a college degree?

Helen was born in 1902. She was the second of four children born to Matilda and Wilson, a farmer of little means. One Sunday he decided not to attend church since he had no money to put in the collection plate. Instead, he walked into the forest with his double-barreled shotgun. Arriving home from church, his wife and children couldn't find him in the house. They searched the forest and discovered him seated beneath a tree with a bullet hole in his head. They could not determine whether the gun had gone off accidentally or whether he had shot himself over his financial problems. He left his family with no income.

Helen's mom was desperate. She married a man who had lost his legs due to diabetes and alcoholism. It wasn't long before he started chasing Helen around in his wheelchair. To keep her safe from sexual abuse, Matilda sent Helen to live with the Cook family, a wealthy Medina couple with two children. Helen helped with the cooking, cleaning, and child care. The Cooks soon realized Helen was capable of furthering her education beyond high school. They paid for her to attend Medina Community College, and she graduated with a business degree after two years. After raising seven children, her degree eventually paid off.

Helen and Karl married in 1925. Karl worked for a railroad company, and the newlyweds received a free honeymoon trip to Niagara Falls and the beaches of Florida. They lost their first child at birth, but my brother Russ followed. He graduated from Case Western University with a business degree. He was in the Reserve Officer Training Corps in the 1940s. The bombing of Hiroshima had taken place, and Russ's first assignment was in Japan. He brought home the strangest looking dolls for Mom. They had white faces, wore long gowns, and had sticks stuck in their hair. I much preferred my baby doll in a buggy. After completing his tour of duty, Russ returned home to work for Kelvinator Appliances. There he met Denise, the love of his life. Next came sister Annette. She was a beauty nicknamed China Doll. She attended high school at a private Lutheran college in Michigan. There she met John, who was in teachers college and was a star football player. She married him after a short career as an American Airlines stewardess that required her to be a beautiful single woman. Annette became pregnant with twins while my mother was pregnant with me. It must have been interesting to see a forty-five-year-old mother and her twenty-two-year-old daughter pregnant together. Unfortunately, Annette followed her mother's pattern of losing the first child at birth. The twins died after five days. A year later, Annette gave birth to her only son, Mike. We became playmates even though I was his aunt. We are still in contact after sixty years. He has four children and is the foster father to many more.

After Annette came Gary, who was attending Ohio State University and living at home when I was born. He went on to dental school in Cleveland. He was taking a course in anatomy when he accidentally ran over my pet cat in the driveway—perfect for him because he dissected the cat in the basement as an anatomy course project. I was mortified to see my pet in that condition, and the smell was terrible. I hope he received an A in the course. I used to love watching Gary fooling around with his boat engines. He would run them in a garbage can full of water in the backyard. At lunchtime, because I was only three years old, I would use a step ladder to reach the kitchen countertop. I would make Gary a sandwich with a slice of bread and a spoonful of peanut butter and would place a carrot on the side. He told me the meal was delicious, so I kept making it.

Sister Wanda was born with a pickle in her mouth. It was hard to understand her defiant attitude. Rumor had it that her high school boyfriend got another girl pregnant and that Wanda found it hard to forgive and forget. She married Carlson on the rebound. Her ex-boyfriend bought a duplex home. He lived in one half with his wife and children, and Wanda and Carlson lived in the other half with their five children. Sounds like an accident waiting to happen.

Ted was the youngest of the fabulous five but not the least. He was a handsome, robust high school football player. He had an alluring personality that even I noticed at three years old. When he came home from school he would take me by the wrists, swing me over his shoulders, and run around the house like a horse. Mom would scold him, warning that he would break my little wrists.

My brothers and sisters always brought a crowd of friends to our house. When they saw a toddler running to and fro, I was cuddled and adored. I gained a false sense of security that left me unprepared to deal with things to come.

There was about a ten-year span between Ted's birth and the unexpected arrival of Ernest. Mom and Dad tried without success to have a playmate for Ernest. The adoption papers were being prepared when I came along.

Compassionate Ernest became my lifelong buddy. He and I were always paired up, but we had quite different personalities. He was quiet, relaxed, and intellectual, a thinker. I was the opposite, a doer, always on the move. When we walked to school, I was ten feet in front of him, turning around only to tie his shoes. When we returned from school, we were supposed to go to Mrs. Murphy's house on days when Mom wasn't home. Ernest had a better idea, as he always did. We went home and he pushed me through the milk shoot, skinny as I was. I opened the door for him. We stuffed ourselves with peanut butter and graham crackers and then went to Mrs. Murphy's to watch the Mouseketeers.

At other times, with three older brothers and a sister around the house to babysit Ernest and me, Mom took the opportunity to manage a church- sponsored store in downtown Cleveland to help the disadvantaged.

CHAPTER 2

Camelot

Even as a four-year-old child, I realized that my house looked very similar to the castle where Cinderella grew up. I lived in a neighborhood where all the houses were owned by upper-class people.

Walking through the front entrance, I stepped into a vestibule with a cobblestone floor, a chandelier, and a coat closet. The next room I called a ladies' hat room. Here women could sit down at a mirror and a vanity, put their hats on a post, and comb their hair. The living room had multiple components. There was a Steinway piano in a cubbyhole, a circular sofa and a round, red-leather table in a huge bay window seating area, a fireplace encompassing an entire wall, and most important, a brand-new television next to a long sofa. There was a little girl's picture over the sofa. I always thought it was me until I saw the same picture in a gift shop thirty years later.

I knew I lived in a special house because in 1949 we had an automatic dishwasher. The dining room table could seat twenty people, which wasn't enough room for all my brothers and sisters with their mates and friends. The dining room was a slice of heaven with a pad of butter on top. It was where family and friends prayed and ate together and celebrated God's grace.

My family was devoutly Lutheran. Almost every Sunday the

pastor and his wife would join us for lunch. Ernest and I would set the table— wineglasses for the adults and thimbles for Ernest and me. The Lutheran prayer book, *Portals of Prayer*, was read after each meal, and you didn't dare leave before then. I didn't understand the stories. I watched the expressions on the faces of the people around the table. At first, they looked sad and then happy, so I guessed they were also glad to leave the table and go outside to play. Mom would read me Bible stories about Noah's ark, Daniel in the lions' den, and baby Jesus in a manger. They were fun to listen to just like the fairy tales about Little Red Riding Hood or Snow White and the Seven Dwarfs. I put them all in one category: not real. I had a long way to go on my journey with God. Looking back, I realize God was always with me. Later, He had to give me a bumpy road so I would hold His hand and not fall.

I was lucky to have so many brothers and sisters to take care of me. That's why my nickname was Lucky. I also was lucky to have a friend called Betsy. She had a pretty black face and a big smile. She would take a bus from downtown Cleveland Monday through Friday to visit me. Betsy had a closet in the kitchen where she kept the black dress and the white apron that she wore in my house. She also kept her dust cloths and vacuum cleaner in the closet. Every time she opened the closet door I could smell the oil-soaked dust cloths.

When Mom went to the church store, Betsy would braid my hair and get me ready for the day. After a while, she didn't come anymore, so Mom would take me to the store with her. Maybe I sensed it, but it wasn't long before Mom told me she had gotten a note in the mail saying Betsy had died. My heart was broken. Little did I know that the many broken hearts to come could not be mended by me, only by God.

It was fun to go downtown with Mom. There were lots of

black kids playing in the alley next to the store. They had never seen a little white girl with long blonde ringlets. They would take a break from their sticks-and-cans game to touch my hair. I thought their game was very much like cricket in my backyard except they didn't have grass to plant the wire stakes. The kids would take me to their homes to show me to their families. Their grandmas and grandpas, aunts and uncles, moms and dads, and brothers and sisters all wanted to touch my hair. They were very loving people.

I had fun with the kids in my neighborhood too. There was an empty wooded lot in back of my house. The neighborhood kids made trails through the trees. The boys had a fort where they kept their toy trucks and cars, and the girls found a patch of wild violets to make a place for their buggies with dolls.

One day, Ernest climbed a tree with very few leaves. He was high up when he grabbed a limb that broke. He came flying down, hitting dead branches along the way. He landed on the ground with a bloody face. I ran for Mom. The doctor showed up with his black bag. He found a needle and thread and stitched Ernest's lip and chin. Maybe he stitched him too tightly, because for the rest of Ernest's life his lower lip drooped over his chin.

CHAPTER 3

Daddy's Little Girl

Dad dressed in a black suit, white shirt, black tie, and wing-tipped shoes every day. I didn't know where he was going, but he sure looked good. I later learned he was an entrepreneur, always starting and ending businesses and going from rich to poor. I knew when he had been out of town, because he always brought me a gift. I particularly remember a forget-me-not teacup and a red clock with a ballerina dancer twirling on top to the tune of "Somewhere over the Rainbow."

My dad's occupation explains why my mom started working in 1956. Dad was ending one business and starting another, selling aluminum awnings for homes and businesses. There was also a demand for ornamental columns to support the awnings. To increase sales, Dad put Mom in charge of the ornamental iron department while he concentrated on making awning sales. Now she could put her college degree in business administration to work.

With both of them working, Mom and Dad were concerned that Ernest and I needed parental guidance. The first five children had left home because they were married and had careers. It was a good idea to combine home and business, so my parents bought a large house with office space in the rear. It was located on a high hill with plenty of land for expansion. Mom eventually built two warehouses for welding and storage. The extra-wide driveway accommodated the sixteen-wheel trucks bringing iron shipments from Louisville, Kentucky. The house was located on a commercial street visible to the public. Mom decorated it with white iron shutters around the windows, iron columns holding up one of Dad's awnings, railings on the front porch, and even wrought iron lawn furniture. An appropriate sign along the road read, "Ornamental Iron House."

Mom became the largest ornamental iron dealer in the Cleveland area. She sold the business to her accountant in 1985. Apparently, he knew the business was a money maker. As of 2016, it was still in operation.

As young as we were, Ernest and I had to toe the line. I did most of the housework and Ernest mowed the acre lot. On days off from school, we worked with Mom in the office. My pretend title was chief advertisement adviser. I put out quarterly mailings and local brochures. Ernest was a little older, so he was dubbed chief office manager. His job included everything from answering the phone to helping customers. Starting a new business was tough. Any profit went back into the business. There were no paychecks then. I later learned that Mom kept a ledger, recording all the hours I worked with no pay. After I was married she gave me full payment in return. Smart mom! I worked out of concern for the family, not for money.

We worked as a family to survive. Remember that thrift shop my mother volunteered to run for the church? That's where I got my school wardrobe. To make extra money, I made potholders on a loom and sold them door to door in the neighborhood. When the going gets tough, the tough get going. These were happy times, with the family working, living, and loving together.

Mom and Dad were definitely right to combine the house with the business, because kids do silly things. As a twelve-year-old, I had the brain of an ant in the body of a five-foot-nine woman. I didn't know that I had grown twelve inches in a year. I thought I could jump over a stool in the basement, but at my height my head hit a steel beam in the ceiling. I must have grabbed my head as I fell to the floor. I ran to the office to show Mom my bloody hands. She looked at the blood gushing from my head and applied a metal ice cube tray to stop the bleeding. Two towels were already blood soaked. Ernest, my sensitive brother, ran for his camera.

This was the one and only time Mom closed the office. She took me to a hospital emergency room. It was a feat to get the metal tray unstuck. I have to hand it to her; she stopped the bleeding and numbed my head while the doctors shaved my head and stitched me up. The doctors asked me if I had lost consciousness. Fortunately, I had not. Had that been the case, I would have bled to death without being found.

When I look back, I know it was a miracle that I survived, but I didn't think miracles happened in real life. Miracles happened only in biblical times to prove that the gospel was true before the New Testament was written. As a twelve-year-old, I had a long way to go on my faith walk with God. Miracles don't happen unless you believe in them. Now that I'm older and wiser, I have had many more miracles happen in my life.

The accident made Mom think about my self-image. I was tall and putting on the pounds. My sister Wanda used to call me an Amazon. That really helped! Mom enrolled me in a dance class, which included baton twirling, ballet, and modern jazz. Again, Mom was the smart one. In one year, I went from an ugly duckling to a graceful swan. I joined with four other girls and did a dance routine in the high school auditorium. I spun around in a not-so-graceful turn, knocked over the table holding the record player, and continued dancing. I guess I exaggerated. I wasn't a swan yet. Mom stepped in to teach me how to walk and stand like a lady. Then I looked like her.

Just after my head injury, I completed eight years in a Lutheran elementary school. At that age, my biggest concern was the bald spot on top of my head. I wore large headbands for about a year before my hair grew long again. I did silly things. I was sometimes reluctant to attend church with my family. I put on my baby blue cashmere coat with the white rabbit fur collar, a white rabbit fur hat, white gloves, and blue pump shoes. Mom would tell me how beautiful I looked as I strolled out of my bedroom. She didn't know I was wearing my pajamas underneath.

There was another good reason to have our home and office together. Remember the black Steinway piano in the living room of Camelot? Now it was by the office door in our new home. Mom hired a piano teacher to come to our house once a week. I'll never forget her. She was tall and thin with long black hair. She wore toothpick dresses, high heels, and lipstick bigger than her lips. I'll bet she was a real babe at a piano bar. She could play anything from ragtime to waltzes, from rock to classics. She taught me everything. Mom would open the office door to hear the lessons. During the week, I would practice every day and Mom would listen. The more she listened, the more I practiced. She would tell me how beautiful the music sounded and how happy it made her feel.

After nine years of lessons, my teacher asked if I would help her by instructing her new pupils. My defining hour came when I appeared in the Cleveland Performing Arts Center. I was the featured pianist, playing "Malaguena" by Ernesto Lecuona. Miss America had played the same song for her talent presentation. When I told Mom, she agreed that we sounded the same on the piano but said we didn't look the same. Imagine that! So she taught me to sit up straight at the piano and to hold my head up high. Again, she was smart!

During this time, I attended Trinity Lutheran Church's catechism class for one year before my confirmation. I became more interested in God's message through the Bible. The minister taught me Christian creeds, the Lord's Prayer, and the Ten Commandments, and believe it or not, I could recite all the books of the Bible, Old Testament and New Testament, in one minute. The Lutheran catechism provided Bible passages that answered my questions about faith in God. One thing was missing: knowing Jesus. I guess I didn't need Him yet. Little did I know what was to come in my life.

I was confirmed in the Lutheran Church in 1958. At just about the same time Ted graduated from Concordia Lutheran Teachers College in Chicago. As a member of the football team, he was physically fit. This may have been a factor in his calling. Graduates received a call for school placement in line with their abilities. Ted's call was to the highlands of New Guinea. All I knew about New Guinea was from *National Geographic* magazine, which depicted the natives' lifestyle. The lowland natives were headhunters whereas the highland natives were much more civilized. Their wealth was determined by the number of pigs they owned.

Ted's call was to start in three months and he would stay in New Guinea for five years. He asked his girlfriend if she would go overseas with him. Vivacious Vicky bought a wedding gown and they were married a few weeks later. It's hard to know what to expect in a foreign country. They were entering the unknown. Medical care was not available. Consequently, Ted and Vicky lost their first child at birth. They had a second child overseas who survived.

Ted's responsibilities included translating English reading, writing, and arithmetic textbooks into pig Latin, the local language. Primarily, he spread God's words of saving grace to the natives. For almost a year, he and Vicky were the only white people in the area until a pastor and his wife arrived to assist. Before Ted's five-year term was completed, he had built a schoolhouse and a church.

Back home in the good old USA, I found it hard to understand the depth of Ted and Vicky's commitment to serve God. Upon their return to America, Ted enrolled in St. Louis Lutheran Theological Seminary. Hearing about their experiences with the natives, I began to realize the importance of loving my neighbors, who lived anywhere in the world, and telling them about God's saving grace.

Ted served as a Lutheran minister in Los Angeles for twenty-five years before he was diagnosed with pancreatic cancer. I likened him to the apostle Paul, who said, "I don't know which I prefer, to die and be with Jesus Christ or live to tell the story of Jesus Christ to nonbelievers." Ted lived seven years after his diagnosis. He was fortunate to be able to minister to all the Missouri Synod Lutheran churches in America. He would write about his illness and about how he found faith, strength, and hope in eternal life. He got both his wishes.

Lutheran schools were academically challenging for me. Mom and the teacher thought I was smarter than I really was, so I started school early and was a year younger than my first-grade classmates. That made a big difference at that age. While the other children were reading Dick and Jane books, I was stumbling along on phonics. The teacher had me read in front of the class as an example of how not to read. That was back when teachers disciplined with a ruler and not with their hearts.

I also attended a Lutheran high school. The academic program was geared toward high-achieving college-bound students. In those days, career goals were different for boys and girls. Boys had a wide range of careers available to them. On the other hand, if a girl was headed for college she had two choices. Do she want to be a nurse or a teacher? Many girls opted to learn secretarial skills or home economics to prepare to be housewives.

My dad was determined that I would be in the college prep program, which included algebra, geometry, trigonometry, biology, chemistry, and Latin. As a consequence, I was an average student. More significant for my life were the friendships I developed in my teens. My best friend today was my best friend when I was twelve years old. It's been said that opposites attract, but I believe otherwise. Sally and I were two peas in a pod. We were both tall and thin with similar facial features and blonde hair. We did not join cliques, and we tried to be friendly to everyone. We got attention from boys, but we were very selective.

Sally and I were in high school when Ernest was attending Ohio State University Business School. He would introduce us to his dormitory friends when we came to see an Ohio State football game. I was so proud of Ernest when he played the bass drum in the marching band at halftime. He also belonged to a rock band that played at fraternity parties and local restaurants. When he did that, Sally and I would bring his complete drum set to his dorm and take it back home. What a perk! The college boys would ask us to dance, and when our high school had a dance we invited our college friends, sparking jealousy from the other girls.

I enrolled in Ohio State University Teaching School in 1962. College was much easier than a private high school. I not only got good grades but became known for my integrity, ambition, and congenial personality. I was recommended for a seat in the Stoic Society, an organization for outstanding students. Like most first-year college coeds, I was also interested in joining a sorority, as were my roommates. I was asked to join the Tri-Sig sorority,

but pledging didn't agree with me. The members did mean, ugly
things to pledges. I spent much of my time with a boyfriend, who
was attending Ohio State Architectural School just three miles
away. Dad didn't like him much because his mother was divorced
and he wasn't a Lutheran.

At this time, Dad was raising money to build five more
Lutheran high schools in the Cleveland area. As the foundation's
founder, he was very influential in the Lutheran Church. He
became friends with the controller of the largest General Motors
assembly plant in the area and solicited him for contributions to
the high school fund. This man had a nineteen-year-old son, who
was bound for Harvard University. We were introduced, but I
wasn't interested. The young boy, Lucas, became friends with my
dad—or more accurately, used my dad to get to me.

The strategy worked. One night, Dad drove up to my college
dorm and told me I was not to see my boyfriend from Ohio State
again. I was to give back his fraternity pin. Lucas and Dad had
made an arrangement. Dad was such a smart man. Why would
he look at people from the outside and not from the inside at
their hearts?

My dad seemed to be getting tired more often. I would see
him go to bed early after reading his Bible. He collapsed at work
and was taken to the hospital for tests. He was diagnosed with a
stroke on the right side of his brain. He was put on blood thinners
and given physical therapy. When I was home from college on a
summer break, Dad's therapist trained me to massage his left arm
and leg to keep them in motion. Defeated! Nothing worked. Now
Dad was losing his ability to think.

In a last-ditch effort, Mom took him to the University of
Michigan Research Hospital where he was diagnosed with
astrocytoma, brain cancer. Mom and my older brothers and
sisters went to the hospital during his brain surgery while I stayed

home, waiting anxiously. I'm a busy bee, so I scrubbed the whole basement floor in our ranch house to calm my nerves—square tile by square tile, inch by inch, all the while asking God for help. This was the first time I had depended on God for help. I sincerely begged Him to save my father. I turned to God when I faced trouble but didn't thank Him when I was blessed. What a selfish person! I needed to improve my relationship with God. This was a turning point in my faith journey.

The brain surgeon opened up Dad's head and closed it back up. The cancer had spread too far. When Dad regained consciousness, I rushed to the hospital. I saw our pastor leaving the hospital, and he told me, "Your dad is gravely ill." He was awake when I entered his room. He asked me what I was going to do. I promised him I would marry Lucas. My fate was sealed. I had made a promise to Dad on his deathbed.

Mom brought him home to die. She called me at the dormitory to come home where I saw Dad, who by then had gone to heaven. When Dad died, I wasn't mad at God. Maybe He was mad at me for doubting Him. My mother always said to tell God, "I do believe. Help my unbelief." The church was filled with Lutherans from far and wide for Dad's funeral. I was trembling and feeling sorry for myself until I saw Grandma walk to the casket and look at her son. No mother should lose a child. Little did I know that I would someday suffer the same loss.

Hoping to comfort her, I stayed with Mom for a few weeks before returning to college. I would wake up in the spare bedroom and hear her wailing in the night. All Ernest and I could do for her was give her a poodle for company. That dog became her best companion in her later years.

PART II

A SCOOP OF HELL

CHAPTER 4

In-laws Should Be Called Outlaws

Getting to know Lucas's parents explained a lot about who he was. An old saying advises, "If you want to know what your girlfriend will look like in forty years, just look at her mother." I can rephrase that. If you want to know how your boyfriend will treat you in forty years, just look at his mother. I looked at Lucas's mom and dad inside and out.

His father got a job transfer from Cleveland to Akron, Ohio. His mother did not want to go, but Lucas's dad insisted. She got back at him, making life miserable for him on his new job. She would not speak to Lucas's father for twenty-five years and seldom did after that. She spoke more frequently to the dog. Lucas's mom played favorites with her children. She was obsessed with Lucas but disenchanted with her daughter, who felt the hate. If you got her angry she wouldn't forget it for the rest of her life.

With a slice of heaven in my hand, I found it difficult to digest this scoop of hell. I wanted to stay away, which made Lucas angry. He said that if I didn't marry him he would drink himself to death. That threat made me feel guilty. He meant that I would be responsible for his death. In retrospect, I see that he said this to control me. That alone should have been a red flag, warning me of danger ahead. Maybe I thought college guys drank a lot and came to their senses later in life, but I should never have assumed that. The drinking increased and so did the threats.

CHAPTER 5

Love from Vietnam?

My wedding took place six months after Dad's death. My oldest brother, Russ, walked me up the aisle. I came back down the aisle with Lucas (henceforth known as BSS, Beloved Son of Satan). What had I done? The tears came down like Niagara Falls. For years, I would cry during the night until I asked God to take control of my life. This part of my story is very difficult to think about, let alone to write. Telling others what happened to me is embarrassing, but I will do that if I can help people in the same situation. Looking back, I can see what I should have done differently to prevent a life in turmoil.

After BSS graduated from Harvard University he was hired by General Motors as a financial analyst. He was fast-tracked to be a future manager. This would require him to travel to General Motors plants around the world. He didn't much care for that idea and refused the position. He used me as a scapegoat, saying I refused to travel. It then appeared I was responsible for his failed career.

I was in turmoil in 1965 and so was America with the escalating war in Vietnam. The army was drafting eligible single men, and it wasn't long before married men were also subject to the draft. I pointed out that enrolling in a master's degree program would mean a deferment, but BSS rejected that idea, preferring to join the army. He was off to boot camp in Missouri, leaving me pregnant and living in a rental duplex. I returned home to live with Mom. I could depend on her for help. I was ashamed that I couldn't be more responsible, but I had nowhere else to turn. I had no job, no money, and a baby on the way. Mom gave me excellent care.

It was a relief when my husband was stationed at the Pentagon near Washington, DC. I went there to have the baby because there were excellent army hospitals in the area. The doctor who delivered baby Andy was stationed at Walter Reed hospital in Washington. We lived in an apartment off base. Leaving the apartment, I fell down a flight of steps, boom, boom, boom on my rear end. Sure enough, Andy was born one month early. My husband dropped me off at the hospital at 11:00 p.m. after my water broke. The doctors told him to go home and wait for a phone call. What was he thinking in taking this advice? We didn't have a phone.

Andy arrived at 4:30 a.m. the next day. When I heard my newborn baby cry, I thanked God for giving me this bundle of joy. Only He could have created this little miracle. I counted all of Andy's fingers and toes. His foot was bent to the leg with the skin stretched tight. I had to rotate the foot every day to bring it back into place, just a minor problem. I thought it was curious that my husband had not called or returned to the hospital after nine hours.

Military hospitals back in 1967 kept moms and newborns for one week. Moms attended classes on nurturing and caring for newborns. Good idea! Most of the new mothers were younger than I was, and I was only twenty-one. Most of us were displaced, moving from one military base to another, with no nearby family or friends. I would call my mom in Cleveland for advice about Andy's colic and other concerns.

The day I brought Andy home from the hospital a woman who lived in an apartment across the parking lot came over to see me. I thought she wanted to see the baby, but instead she told me that my husband had been with a girl in a first-floor apartment the night Andy was born. They had a pizza delivered to the apartment. That was interesting. He never bought me a pizza, claiming he had no money. Maybe I was naive but I couldn't believe he was cheating on me. If he needed someone to talk to, he might have been wiser to see the elderly woman on the second floor. In retrospect, I shouldn't have been so trusting. In the next chapter I recall the ultimate cheating story. I should have gotten the message that day about what was ahead for me, but I was a dependent with a new baby and no job.

That night, Andy woke up crying. I tried to get up to take care of him, but BSS held me down in the bed and said, "No child is going to control me." Baby Andy and I cried until there were no tears left. I can't explain why I didn't get up and leave my husband. I was in disbelief that anyone could treat a baby and a mother with such disdain.

I didn't know if it was fear of the Vietnam War or the responsibility of a newborn baby that caused by husband's depression. We went on a picnic and he spilled the beans in more ways than one. He said he couldn't think clearly because he had disturbing thoughts in his head. This was the first of only two times that he admitted a psychological problem. His mother had a significant influence on his behavior. It's safe to call her BMS (Beloved Mother of Satan).

That picnic conversation may have caused my miscarriage. I lost the baby in the toilet. I guessed from the fetal development that I must have been three months pregnant. I was amazed at how well developed the fetus was at that stage. I couldn't help but wonder how some people could choose to abort such a precious gift of life. I went to the hospital for a D&C (dusting and cleaning) operation to stop the bleeding. My husband stopped by to visit me. I asked, "Where's baby Andy?" He said, "In his crib at home." In a panic, I said, "Go home and take care of him."

I thought that after one year and six months in the military, BSS had escaped a tour of duty in Vietnam. But sure enough, with just six months left in the service he was shipped there. In retrospect, I wonder if he had volunteered. I entered the revolving door at Mom's house. Annette's son, Mike, and Ernest were also there, helping Mom in the business for the summer. I was delighted. Now Andy had two great guys to teach him how to talk, crawl, and walk. They were dependable babysitters when I went off to work at the local department store for extra income.

I prepared for BSS's return by purchasing a small beginner house. My father-in-law helped with the purchase and painted all the walls while I cleaned and furnished the place. BSS's return was bittersweet. Little Andy had his daddy back, but BSS brought me an unwanted present. After a few weeks I found genital warts on me. I saw the same on him. Why didn't he tell me about his problem? Didn't he care if he infected me? It was time for him to come clean in more ways than one.

My husband said he went to Singapore for a week on R&R (rest and relaxation). There he found a prostitute, supposedly US-regulation clean. I may or may not have believed that. I knew young Vietnamese women went to army bases to wash clothes for the soldiers. Since BSS brought home a picture of her, I suspected she was significant in his life. I knew wives could be invited to meet their husbands at R&R sites, but I did not receive that invitation. Instead BSS brought me back a present. He was in Vietnam for only six months. I guess I was out of sight, out of mind.

After his explanation, I asked him, "If you love me how could

you do this to me?" His answer brought the deepest hurt of my
life. He said, "I guess I didn't love you enough." What had I done
wrong that I didn't deserve to be loved? If he didn't love me, why
was he holding me in bondage? Maybe he couldn't care less about
me, because he didn't give me the consideration to protect me
from his disease.

What would I do now? My first thought was to divorce an
unfaithful husband. On second thought, I had no money, no job,
and a brand-new baby. I was too embarrassed to tell relatives or
friends about my problem. I would ruin my family's reputation.
How could I cope with my life? Who could I talk to? Then I
remembered God's words in Matthew 6:25: "Therefore I tell you,
do not worry about your life, what you will eat or drink or your
body, what you will wear. Is not life more than food and the body
more than clothes?" Matthew 6:27 says, "Who of you by worrying
can add a single hour to his life span?" Matthew 6:28 assures us
that if God cares for the lilies of the field, we, who are so much
more, need not worry.

If God loved people that much, He would be with me and
would protect me. Jesus Christ would always walk with me and
talk with me and tell me that I was His own. Through prayer, I
expressed feelings that I kept inside. I was deeply hurt by someone
who had promised to love me. My trust in another human being
had been betrayed. I knew I had to forgive or I would become
hateful and bitter. That would be no way to raise my two-year-
old child.

I dedicated my life to honor God above all and to love my
neighbor as myself. There was no room for hate, but there was
room for explanations. If you sense that your mate has a wandering
eye it's best to clear the air right away. The infidelity will probably
happen again but with greater consequences. It happened to me.
The same goes for physical abuse. If you are hit one time, chances

are that bridge has been crossed and you will be hit again. And never put up with name calling. If you allow yourself to be called a jerk or an asshole that will be your name for life. Avoid being a controller's victim. Seek intervention and begin changing the wrong to right.

CHAPTER 6

Stop Crying and Make Something of Yourself

My crying and sadness took a toll on my health. I lost another baby. I waited too long to get to the hospital. I lost all feeling in my arms and legs from losing too much blood. Again, the hospital fixed me up with a D&C operation. You may be wondering why I would have sexual relations with a man I feared. I desperately wanted a large family. I had experienced that slice of heaven in my childhood and wanted to enjoy it again. Mom would always say, "It's a shame to have only one child." Make no mistake, there is a big difference between making love and having sex to procreate. In childbearing years and after, if you are ignored when you say no, you've been raped, and being married doesn't change that fact.

Mentally and physically I became very weak. I was diagnosed with viral pneumonia. The doctor gave me a choice, go to bed or to the hospital. What was I to do with a little boy who needed to be picked up from first grade at a private school five miles away? BSS could take him to school. We asked BMS, Beloved Mother of Satan, to bring him home. Ungenerous person that she was, it took her only a few days to tell me, "Get out of bed and take care of your own child."

As soon as I did, I got pleurisy, a tearing of the lungs' lining, and was sentenced to six more weeks in bed. I could walk only to the bathroom and back to bed. My ankles were itchy and appeared to have sores on them. I thought my medication was to blame. As I shuffled about, I noticed little bugs flying out of the carpet. I discovered dead insects on the windowsills and saw my cute little toy poodle scratching himself. The house and the dog were not being cleaned, but I had to deal with that problem another day.

With pneumonia, I lost the desire to eat. After a few months, I was hungry enough to get out of bed and make soup. I walked to the kitchen stove, looked about me, and commented that the floor was dirty. BSS was sitting at the kitchen table with a beer in his hand. "You think this kitchen floor is dirty?" he said. "I'll show you dirty." He poured his beer all over the floor and said, "Now that's dirty. Clean it up, bitch." I did.

Life can be very simple without a car. I would put Andy in a wagon and take him down to the dime store two blocks away. My neighbors were all working, and I didn't see any of them during the week. Sunday was the only day I saw adults. When BSS returned home from work at 5:00 p.m., I liked to talk about little, everyday things. Then one evening I got his message loud and clear. "I'm extremely tired," he said. "I've been conversing all day. The last thing I want to do is hear your voice or talk to you."

This was the day my life changed for the better. I stopped feeling sorry for myself and started making something of myself. The ranch house I had bought had a large basement where I could retreat when BSS came home. As a young girl, I had gotten a sewing machine, and now I could put it to use. The house needed curtains, so I put Andy in the wagon and pulled him to the dime store where I bought cotton material. My newly made café curtains looked great throughout the house. I made dresses for church. I even made a lined suit. With Andy at my side, we could make a real mess. He liked to pull the thread off the spools.

My sister Annette collected pine cones, little bitty ones and great big ones, and I used them to make pine cone wreaths for every season of the year. My favorite creation was a mixed-nut wreath with each nut sealed in Saran Wrap. These were gifts for relatives and friends on holidays.

My other sister, Wanda, gave me her coral-colored bedroom set for Andy's transition from a crib to a twin bed. I thanked her very much but learned how to strip furniture and painted the set colonial blue. Next, I taught myself how to upholster chairs and sofas. I was led to believe that there was no money available for frivolous decorating. I learned to make something out of nothing. For example, I upholstered a a Queen Ann chair with a fabric scrap and refinished the wood with a can of cherry stain.

On my wagon walks with Andy, I noticed that the savings and loan next to the dime store was advertising for a part-time teller. The bank was only three blocks away, so I wouldn't need a car. I asked my husband if I could apply for the position. Surprise! I got the job.

My first day began at 9:30 a.m. and ended at 4:30 p.m. I walked one block down a busy street and then started down my street, Whispering Lane. I sensed I was being followed. Looking around, I saw a young man in a jalopy stalking me. As I neared my house, I decided to turn around and walk back to the main street. I didn't want him to know where I lived. If I opened my door, he could follow me inside. I walked to the dentist's office where Andy and his dad had an appointment, and I drove home with them. If I was to keep this job, I in fact needed a car. That night we bought a yellow Chevy Nova. BSS was a General Motors executive and cars didn't cost him too much money.

As a teller, I was honest, accurate, and much admired by

the bank manager because my drawer money was never out of balance. Not so with the other tellers. At the end of the day, if a teller was out of balance we all had to stay and find the error. On one such occasion, I was late picking up Andy at my mother-in-law's. She was taking care of him until I left work. When I arrived, she told me to stay home and take care of my own child. Now you know where my husband got his pleasant personality.

I sure did like my car. I enrolled in afternoon classes at Akron University. I never did receive my undergraduate degree after I was married and my husband was drafted. I decided to enroll in a few business classes to expand my horizons in the banking industry.

I have always been a faithful Lutheran Church attendant. When Andy was four years old, I enrolled him in the preschool Sunday school class. I loved being around twenty-five to thirty small children so much that I volunteered to teach in the program. After seven years, I was asked to be the preschool director. One of my responsibilities was to order and to sort the story and art projects into age levels. In my handy-dandy basement, I created a Sunday school workshop center. I had the world at my fingertips and God as my center's director. He and I became creative.

Leaving BSS upstairs by himself was like leaving a puppy dog home alone. When it was time for bed, I would tiptoe up the steps to find him slumped over his chair. He'd sit in his chair, urinate, and spill beer all over. At least he enjoyed himself.

CHAPTER 7

The Lord Gives and the Lord Takes

Annette, who lived in Illinois with her husband, John, and son, Mike, loved to visit. Mom and I were happy to have her. My sister was so much fun to be with, but I noticed her health was deteriorating. None of my illnesses could compare with what Annette was going through at forty-one. She was diagnosed with ovarian cancer that had spread to other organs, and death was imminent. Mom opened up her revolving door one more time and brought a bedridden Annette home to die.

Annette lived several months with Mom. Thank goodness Mom had sold the business and could take care of her. I came to Annette's bedside to sit with her and to console her. I wanted to say a prayer with her, but I wasn't able to express my deep fear of losing her. I asked God in my heart to take away her pain by taking her to heaven to be with Him.

Nothing could have prepared me for that final moment. When Mom called me on a Saturday afternoon to say that Annette had passed, I came over immediately with BSS and Andy. The undertaker was already there. Annette was lying in the same position in which I had last seen her, but she had stopped breathing. When Dad had died I heard Mom wailing every night. I knew she was suffering now. No mother should lose a child.

Annette was cremated and buried in the cemetery with her twins and her father.

During this time, I was pregnant again. After two miscarriages, I wanted this baby to survive. I had made it through the first trimester and well into the second when I began experiencing labor pains at home. They continued at the hospital. At the beginning, because of the possibility of losing the baby, I was given no medication to help with childbirth. The baby wasn't helping because it was dead.

The experience was very difficult, not only physically but psychologically. My gynecologist wanted to get to the bottom of my problem. Months later, he injected dye into my reproductive system. Pictures showed no problems. This test gave me more confidence in my ability to have a normal child.

I was still working as a bank teller when baby Alex arrived. He was born at eight months. I was at Mom's home with the revolving door having lunch, and BSS was waterskiing on a nearby lake, free as a lark. When I got home my water broke. Soon after, BSS arrived home and took me to the hospital. Andy, now nine years old, ran around the neighborhood proclaiming the good news.

The next morning, still no baby. Alex was smarter than all of us. He took one look at us sad sacks and decided he didn't want to join us.

Little Alex was induced to come out the next day. Instantly, BSS left for work. You might think he would stick around to enjoy the moment. My vital signs were being monitored. The doctors were slowly losing me. I was put in a private room with a heart specialist at my side for eight hours until my heart resumed a normal beat. I had previous heart defects, so I wasn't surprised. Again, BSS wasn't there for me in childbirth.

CHAPTER 8

First Finger Surgery

You may assume I was a loner, but that was not the case. I kept my childhood friends and made new friends along the way. They were and still are supportive, encouraging, and faithful. My friends have been by my side since high school and college days. My family friends were brothers Gary and Ernest. It's been said you can pick your friends but not your relatives. I disagree. My brothers and sisters have been my mentors and my idols.

When I invited my friends over to the house they became the friends BSS didn't have. One evening, I had three couples over for snacks. With us, that was eight people, but I had only four everyday plates. I resurrected a wedding gift of twelve crystal plates. When BSS saw them set out, he kicked in the table, saying, "Who do you think you're trying to impress?" As usual I had no comment. To challenge him would only intensify his anger, and he would be more violent. The next morning, it was business as usual. He drank so much he couldn't remember what he did the night before.

I wasn't a loner but I was lonely for a loving husband and a house full of children. God knew better. This was not a good marriage in which to create a family. I faced many challenges at home. BSS did not call me a Christian woman but a jerk and an asshole who could do nothing right. He blamed me for things beyond my control. When a faucet leaked, it was my fault for pushing the lever too hard. Normally, I would not respond, but this time, in my defense, I told him I felt certain I didn't have the strength to do that.

This ailment came on very slowly, starting with finger aches when I held a cold hose while watering the grass. Eventually, my lower knuckles enlarged and bent my fingers in a ninety-degree angle. My pointer finger developed arthritic cysts that broke the skin, leaving open sores. My doctor said nothing could be done for chronic arthritis except medication. I did not want to take that approach since a girlfriend who had arthritis at thirty-eight took too much medication and died from a bleeding stomach.

I switched to a hand surgeon. Dr. Joint removed a knuckle bone from the finger with arthritic cysts and replaced it with a screw. After that I called him Dr. Payne. There are lots of nerve endings in digitals, and my finger was throbbing. That explains the Chinese torture of bamboo splints under the nails. I called the surgeon Dr. Marvel when I saw that my beautifully formed, pain-free middle finger didn't bend. When I held it up to show people the results of my surgery, they thought I was giving them the finger.

CHAPTER 9

Everything You Ever Wanted to Know You Learned in Kindergarten

That little starter ranch house was way too small for a baby room. We couldn't even fit the bassinet in the master bedroom. Fortunately, we had several buyers for our doll house. With all the competition, we were offered more money than we were asking.

We wanted to move further out of Cleveland into the Cuyahoga Falls area. Colonial-design two-story homes were more popular in the suburbs. I knew that BSS was a tightwad and that I had to find a fixer-upper in order to afford a home in an upper-middle-class neighborhood. I did! The former owner had six children, two dogs, and grandma living in the dining room. There were four or five motorcycles in the greasy garage.

We had found the perfect house, but I had my work cut out for me. I used my creative skills, painting and wallpapering the whole interior. I had all the carpeting and the tile floors replaced and the kitchen cabinets refinished. That made a huge difference. When I finished cleaning all the cupboards, especially where the dogs ate, it was home. When it came time to sell, we found a buyer in a few days and got much more money than we paid for the house.

There was a Lutheran elementary school within five miles of

our new home, and Andy could take a bus back and forth. The school was looking for a new eighth-grade teacher. Andy told the principal that I had gone to teacher's college and had almost gotten my degree. I was within two classes and teacher practice of graduating. Van, the principal, asked if I could fill in until the school found a certified teacher. I agreed. I taught American literature to eighth-graders three times a week for three months. They particularly liked reading *The Red Badge of Courage* by Stephen Crane. I took eighteen-month-old Alex with me to the preschool. He was far too young to participate in the activities, but the teachers let him attend for a short time.

Occasionally, the principal would sit in and observe my class. This proved to be a defining moment, launching me in a new career. Van told me I was an excellent teacher. If I finished my two remaining courses and student taught by the next fall, he would hire me as the kindergarten teacher. If ever I had a mentor in my life it was Van. I agreed to finish the courses but I had a problem. What was I to do with little Alex? There again Van helped me out. He recommended a woman who babysat ten to twelve children every morning. Alex would be a welcome addition.

I had a new lease on life. Hold on—not too fast. Something was going wrong in my body. My gynecologist found a tumor during an annual exam. After an ultrasound test, he called me into his office and asked me to bring my husband. I heard the worst words of my life. He knew my sister had recently died of ovarian cancer. This appeared to be the same thing, only catching it in time would make the difference. The tumor had grown to the size of a grapefruit. The doctor felt a sense of urgency and wanted me to have surgery within a few days. I was taking college exams that week. I asked if the surgery could be postponed. He said definitely not. He stressed the seriousness of my illness when he told my husband and me to put our affairs in order and to make sure that the children had a caretaker.

It's hard to describe my feelings before the surgery. At best, I felt numb, just going through the motions. I had no thought for the future. That was out of my control. I couldn't ask to live or die. God was in control.

Before leaving for the hospital I found it difficult even to look at the boys for fear I'd cry. I took Alex to the backyard swing and told him, "Good-bye, Sweet Pea." I couldn't tell String Bean (Andy) all the details. He would be too worried. My first concern was finding a babysitter for the children after school until their father got home from work. I asked my mother-in-law if she could watch the children for a few afternoons. She said yes but changed her mind after babysitting the first day. By this time my mother was far too old to handle the children or to drive.

I decided Andy was up to the job. I called him from the hospital to describe the responsibility he had. "In the morning, get your little two-year-old brother up, change his diaper, give him breakfast, make lunches for both of you, and take him on the bus to school. Don't forget to pick him up in the preschool room and bring him home. Then you have to babysit until your dad gets home for dinner." Lots of responsibility for an eleven-year-old. Dear God, how could this be? I couldn't leave the boys with their father for a day. How could I leave them with him for a lifetime?

After the surgery, my Lutheran minister came to the hospital to give me communion. I wondered if he thought he was giving me last rites. I accepted the bread and wine, but I had to confess that I had spoken to Dr. Lifesaver. He had come to my bedside while I was still groggy from anesthesia and said, "You're going to be okay." The tumor was on the uterus and not on the ovary. He had removed the benign uterus, cervix, and appendix. Had my gynecologist misdiagnosed ovarian cancer? I don't think so. He seemed very confident about his diagnosis. I believe in miracles. It wasn't my time to die. God had another plan.

I came home after a week in the hospital but did not get a warm reception. I had a huge incision from hip to hip. I needed bed rest and could do only light tasks for six weeks. That evening, after getting comfy in our bed, I heard BSS tell me to get out and sleep elsewhere. Where was I to go? There were no empty beds in the house. I found a camping cot and put it in the den. I didn't know what was wrong with him. I thought maybe my large scar bothered him.

Shortly after I recovered, for the second time ever BSS asked to talk with me. We went out onto the patio away from the kids in the house. He confessed that something was going wrong with his thinking process. I can't remember how I responded. If I could do it over again, I would ask him about his faith in God. From what I remember, he believed in the Bible but was disenchanted with the organized church. We went to church together, but he would not participate in songs and prayers. Does that matter? The most important thing that God wants us to remember is in the New Testament, John 3:16: For God so loved the world that He gave His only begotten Son that whoever believes in Him will not perish but have eternal life.

BSS was right! Something strange was going on in his head. Here's one example. During summer thunderstorms, he would take Andy, Alex, and me to the basement and herd us into a fruit cellar under the steps. The cellar was about three feet wide and three feet high with shelves on both sides. There was no room to stand up. We took a flashlight because we had to keep the door shut. After repeating the procedure several times, I wondered why I never had to do this as a child. Had the weather in Ohio gotten that bad? One time I sneaked upstairs to see the storm. I found the sun shining and BSS sitting on the front porch smoking a cigarette. Yes, it had rained but not much and not then. Why did we have to stay in the basement? I would never do that again.

When one door is shut, another door is opened. I created workstations in the basement as I had done in my first house. During my six-week recovery I wanted to prepare myself to teach kindergarten in the fall. In my little cubbyhole office, I wrote twelve learning units with themes appropriate for each season. For example, in January we would learn about "our friends, the Eskimos."

The units would include songs, finger plays, art projects, stories, artifacts for the show-and-tell table, and even musical plays with costumes. Other themes were good health habits, careers, Pilgrims and Indians, presidents, and of course, holidays and special events. I also included a unit on Ohio leaves in my lesson plan. The principal was so impressed that he asked me if he could submit my unit to the Concordia Publishing Company. I was honored. In the upcoming school year, every Missouri Synod Lutheran school in America received a copy of my unit.

When the school year began I was well prepared. I had taken eighteen hours of graduate courses in child development at Ohio State University in anticipation of teaching kindergarten. I had also taken graduate courses in creative arts, producing all sorts of learning games, calendars, name tags, and birthday hats and learning age-appropriate songs and finger plays.

I was honored to be the kindergarten teacher at Trinity Lutheran School. I took my responsibilities seriously. Guiding twenty-five five-year-olds through their first year of school was challenging, but the task brought me much laughter and love.

Now I could put my piano playing to good use. The children loved to gather around me and sing along with the music. Sometimes a piano was not available, so I strummed the melodies on a guitar.

I wrote several operettas designed for special events during the school year. For example, the Thanksgiving Day play featured the children dressed as Indians and Pilgrims sitting around a festive dinner table. I especially enjoyed the play on the last day of school when they sang about all the things they had learned in kindergarten. The children were on the stage, and I sat at the piano below in front of them. They listened for the key note and sang to their proud parents.

Parents paid extra money for the personalized education that Trinity, a Christian school, offered their children. At their request, I taught phonics, reading, and math, advanced subjects for kindergartners. Since this was an all-day class, the children had lunch and naps together in the afternoon.

Twenty-five children were ready for the year, but I wasn't. After a few months around children with colds and flu, I couldn't get well. In the final two months of the school year, I was diagnosed with bacterial pneumonia. My good friend Jean, also a schoolteacher, substitute taught for me until the summer break. One Friday morning, she brought the whole class to my driveway, and the children sang to me as I peered out of my upstairs bedroom window. There was always a silver lining in my clouds.

In my third year of teaching, Alex graduated from preschool and moved on to kindergarten. Since his mother was the teacher, he must have made up his mind that he wasn't going to be treated differently from the other kids. Entering the classroom on the first day of school, he said, "Good morning, Mrs. Summers," just like the other kids. He kept his secret for months until one of his classmates asked me, "Are you Alex's mom?" I said yes. I never told Alex that someone knew his secret.

On the first day of class I asked the children to draw a picture of what they remembered about their summer. Most of them drew pictures of a family picnic, a trip to the beach, or fun in the pool. Alex drew a vivid picture of his great-grandmother's funeral. He designed a casket almost as big as his eight-by-eleven-inch sheet of paper. The drawing included details such as the tiny casket wheels supported by accordion legs that could go up or down, scrolls on the casket sides, and a pillow with Grandma's head turned sideways so we could see the frown on her face.

As a kindergarten teacher, I was interested in Alex's exceptional ability to draw details, because it showed his level of maturity. Before I admitted children into the class, I tested their maturity levels in many ways, one of which was to draw a picture of a person. Some children drew details such as fingers and toes, facial expressions, and clothing. Less mature children would draw only a torso, head, arms, and legs. Most of all, I learned how much Alex was affected by death. He had learned the reality of life. It may be true that everything you ever wanted to know you learned in kindergarten. The rest of the class also learned the reality of death from his picture.

CHAPTER 10

Treachery at Sea

I've always loved to be around boats ever since Gary stored his boats in the backyard at Camelot. When he moved to Sand Harbor, Nevada, to become the city dentist, I spent my summers with him on Lake Tahoe. He taught me how to waterski, to row a boat, and to sail a skiff.

When BSS and I were first married, we bought a rowboat for fishing. In typical fashion, the boats got bigger and bigger. Next came a speedboat, even before a second car. I guess the boat penny jar was bigger than the car penny jar. Maybe a boat was more fun than a car. We taught Andy how to water-ski at seven years old. I water-skied until I was fifty-eight. The next boat was a twenty-five-foot sailboat. It was a great idea for the boys to learn how to navigate, to set sails to the wind direction, and to control the boat with wind power.

Our first attempt to sail was canceled. We were packing up for a weekend trip to Catawba Island on our new craft. The night before, I had a 104-degree fever and was coughing up blood. I called my physician, who told me to go to the local hospital. Emergency staff advised that I be admitted. My next choice was to go to an all-night drugstore to get Keflex medication. As we left the hospital, I asked BSS to drive a block away to pick up a prescription. He told me he was way too tired and would get it in the morning. I was afraid I would die before then, but he did get the medicine the next morning. He left on a boat trip with the boys that day. That was okay. I couldn't have gone anyway. It took me several months to recover.

Our next attempt to visit Catawba Island came months later. We had a wonderful time sailing thirty miles across Lake Erie. On our return voyage, we encountered a sailboat traveling in the opposite direction. The people aboard shouted, "Watch the weather." It looked sunny to us. We had no ship-to-shore phone, cell phone, or weather information, so we kept on going. Everyone learned a good lesson: never leave shore without a means of communication.

The winds picked up. I can't tell you the speed because we had no manometer. The rain clouds reached down to pick up the waves and toss them into our cockpit. Alex and I went below to the cabin. He got seasick from the motion of the boat and vomited. Andy tried to steer the boat with the tiller, but the force of the wind broke the steering mechanism. Fortunately, we were driven behind Kelly's Island until the storm passed. The boys learned many lessons on that trip. Chief among them is that following all the rules does no good if the captain is drunk. Boating and drinking don't mix. That's why I have so many tragic stories about sailing the Great Lakes.

BSS replaced the twenty-five-foot sailboat with a twenty-eight-foot sailboat. In hindsight, I should have known this was the beginning of a series of bigger boats and larger beer kegs. There had to be some logic to his madness. How about the bigger the sailboat, the safer the ride? Not so! Here are a few tales of treachery at sea.

Alex, his dad, and I set sail for the south coast of Lake Erie. We had a good time visiting several ports along the way. We sailed into Port Ashtabula on a cloudy, windy day. We were locked in for a few days because of high winds and treacherous seas. On Saturday, BSS said we had to get home for work on Monday regardless of the weather. Big mistake!

We headed out of the channel with the wind on our starboard side and turned to go south with following seas. By our calculations, the waves were more than fifteen feet high at our stern. We could not turn around or we would capsize. We sat in the cockpit, wearing life jackets and watching every wave. The rain poured down, adding to the danger. Our eight-foot dinghy trailed behind the boat until the wind blew it into the cockpit on top of us. I prayed to God, "Please don't let us drown at sea." Alex and his dad took turns at the helm. Their arms and hands were sore from steering. I could not even attempt to hold the steering wheel.

After thirty miles, we sighted Port Mentor. We sent praises up to God until we realized that the port entrance was flanked by concrete walls and that we might well slam into them. We took the chance. If we lost the boat in the channel, at least we could swim to shore. Our prayers were answered. The waves kept us buoyant like a cork and moving enough to keep us off the walls. The next morning, God sent brilliant sunshine and a bright blue sky. We limped into homeport ringing wet and sore-armed but safe.

Afterward, I remembered the Bible story about Jesus crossing the Sea of Galilee with His disciples. Jesus fell asleep in the cabin. After a while, a squall came up. The wind was fierce, the rain poured down, and the tiny boat was tossed about. The disciples woke Jesus and said, "Teacher, don't you care if we drown?" Jesus said to the seas, "Quiet. Be still."

Was Jesus asleep in our cabin? If I had offered Him a life jacket and asked Him to join us in the cockpit, would He have said, "Thank you for remembering Me," and come outside to calm the seas? On second thought, what did the disciples call Jesus? Teacher! Now I understood. Jesus was teaching us a lesson: don't venture out on treacherous seas and expect God to calm them. We used bad judgment and had to take the consequences. We learned that we shouldn't behave foolishly and expect God's grace.

That same boat took us through more than one peril at sea. We entered Sandusky Bay from Lake Erie on a windy day. The waves built as we went from deep to shallow water. The mountain of water behind us came over the cockpit. Sailors call that being pooped on. Safe in port, we stayed two days at a scenic site. Sunday morning, we couldn't get the engine started. Again, the captain said we had to get home for work on Monday. We decided to use the sails for power. Approaching the entrance to Lake Erie, we encountered the same seas. We observed a ferryboat next to us taking on water over the bow. Neither boat could turn back. We had no engine power, but the winds were in our favor and so strong that we sailed all the way to homeport.

Instead of sobering up and making better decisions, BSS bought a bigger boat to handle the waves. He traded in the twenty-eight-foot sailboat for a thirty-four-foot sloop sailboat. Interestingly enough, the day we sold the smaller sailboat, lightning hit the mast, put a hole in the hull, and destroyed all the electrical equipment. Satan must have been on mountain standard time instead of eastern standard time to miss striking the new boat.

By this time, Andy was in college and Alex in high school, so I ventured out to sea alone with the captain. I knew the basics of sailing, but most of the time I was in the galley preparing meals for the crew. Now I was put to the test. We were on Lake Erie, possibly ten to fifteen miles from port. The three-foot waves were whitecapped but not dangerous. The jib and the main sail were full of wind, so we were flying through the waves. The captain, having finished a six-pack of beer, looked at the dinghy trailing behind us and noticed that an oar was loose. He decided to climb into the dinghy, his beer in one hand, and to grab the oar with the other. I yelled, "Don't forget your life jacket."

The warning fell on deaf ears. BSS toppled off of the dinghy into the water. The wind was rapidly taking the boat away from him. With his white hair, I couldn't see him in the whitecaps. I wondered what he was thinking as he watched his boat sail away from him with no land in sight. He knew I had never sailed the boat single-handedly.

I knew I had to get the sails down. Sloop sailboats have large main sails, too big to handle manually. I let the halyard go, and the sails slid down the mast. The boat stopped. Now I had to start the engine, which was difficult because I had to time it perfectly. I pushed the primer button, counted to twenty-five, and pushed the starter button. The engine didn't start. I knew it would flood if I tried too many times. I tried again. Success!

I turned the boat around, trying to follow its wake because I couldn't see BSS. I knew he couldn't survive much longer. I pushed the throttle to full speed. I jokingly thought about his life insurance policy but quickly realized his mom would kill me if I didn't bring him back alive. I found him on the right side of the boat. He cried out, "You damn near ran me over, asshole." So much for gratitude. I turned the boat around, bringing the dinghy close to him so he could grab the side. He hung on for a while until he got the strength to climb in. I wondered how much longer he would have survived in the water.

Our next adventure took us to Lake Huron's North Channel. The water was pristine and surrounded by beautiful pine trees. We came behind Rattlesnake Island in a thunderstorm in time to reach safety. No restrooms were available, so BSS urinated all over the top of the cabin. I got a bucket of water from the lake to rinse it off. He became very angry with me and screamed to Alex that I was a terrible mother. For once, I was blessed that he was so drunk he could not find me in my hiding place. He got tired and fell asleep. The next morning, he didn't remember a thing.

The thirty-four-foot sailboat turned out to be the captain's home on and off in the 1980s. Rumor had it that he often fell off of the dock into the channel. Each time, someone heard the splash and rushed to his rescue. If the marina water hadn't frozen over in some winters, he probably would have got dunked more often.

Spring comes slowly in Ohio, but even in cool weather the Sandusky Yacht Club held events. One year, we were in charge of the St. Patrick's Day dinner. Despite our martial problems, we showed up to fulfill our responsibilities. However, it was hard to hide BSS's drinking problem when he could hardly set the tables after a few afternoon beers. By evening, he was an embarrassment.

After dinner was served and the tables were cleared, BSS asked me if I was going to stay on the boat overnight. On an earlier occasion, I had decided to sleep on the boat instead of driving fifty miles late at night. I said I was going home. He replied, "If you leave me here, I'll get so drunk I will fall off the dock and drown." For the first time in my life I stood up to him and said, "This is the last time you will ever blame me for your behavior." I drove home much relieved that he was there and I was home.

CHAPTER 11

Counselors Helping a Future College Counselor

After the Patrick's Day confrontation BSS stayed on the boat approximately one cold season. Not to worry; the boat had heat. Trying to be a better person, he asked me if I wanted to see a marriage counselor. I agreed. Perhaps someone else could figure out this mess. Tightwad that he was, he knew his health insurance would cover the cost.

Our first marriage counselor was a young man who had no idea how to fix the situation. Our second marriage counselor was a young girl who asked which one of us wanted to tell the story. For the full hour, BSS complained about me. She asked if I had any comments. I said no because I knew he would walk all over me verbally. Now BSS was making progress. He wanted to see more counselors because he could outtalk me. Actually, he was verbally abusing me right in front of the counselor. I was sent to a psychiatrist. He interviewed me and decided he needed to see my husband for analysis.

Next, we tried individual counselors. I didn't know until then that I was able to speak up for myself when BSS was not there. I told my counselor that BSS drank to excess, which caused unexpected anger. He was verbally, emotionally, sexually, and mentally controlling, but at that point he had not been physically abusive. He would tip over tables, lock me out of the bedroom at night which prevented me from getting ready for work in the morning, sleep in the bathtub, and urinate anywhere but in the toilet. After that conversation the counselor said, "You don't need me. Here is the business card of a lawyer you should contact. Run now; run fast. Your husband's a snake in the grass."

BSS decided counseling had gotten him nowhere, so he apologized for his behavior and asked if I would forgive him. I guess he was sorry after living on the boat for a year and more. Should I give him the benefit of the doubt? There was always room for forgiveness. I decided to make one last try before I called the lawyer listed on the business card.

CHAPTER 12

God, Please Don't Take Andy Yet

We went for a boat ride on Lake Erie, anchored, and tied the dinghy to the sailboat's stern where I read a book. I was startled to see a coast guard boat steaming toward me. What kind of trouble could we be in? The coast guard captain asked, "Are you Maggie Summers?" I said yes. He told me to get to port immediately because my son had been critically injured in an accident. I didn't know which son he meant. They were both in the Blue Ridge Mountains. Alex was with his girlfriend and her family white-water rafting in North Carolina, and Andy was with his wife and her family in a mountaintop condo in Tennessee.

While powering to port, we received a call from Carla, Andy's wife. She described the accident. Andy was bicycling down a two-lane mountain road. He was in full gear with helmet, gym shoes, knee and elbow pads, and gloves. The left side of the road was lined with boulders. On the right side, he could see the roofs of houses below. Andy was pedaling down the mountain at thirty miles an hour when a commercial panel truck pulled onto the road in front of him. He couldn't stop. Should he slam into the boulders on the left side or go through the roofs on the right side? He couldn't miss the truck, so he turned his body to the left rather than hit the truck head-on. Crash!

The truck driver called the police, who called an ambulance.

Since the helicopter was in use, Andy could not be airlifted to the hospital. The EMS crew took him to the nearest hospital, which would not admit him. His injuries were too serious. He needed a trauma center. EMS workers sped sixty miles to a trauma center in Knoxville, Tennessee, fearing they would not make it in time. Carla concluded the message by saying, "Andy wants you to come, come quickly. He's glad you are together."

Back on shore, I gathered what belongings I had and headed for the car. BSS said, "Where are you going? We are not leaving until morning. I'm too tired." What if Andy didn't survive until morning? How could BSS make that decision? I didn't understand his thinking process, but I suspected that he was caught off guard and had already had too much alcohol that day and was too tired to drive. I could drive but he would not allow that.

We arrived at the University of Tennessee Hospital the next day in the late afternoon and were just in time to see Andy being wheeled out of surgery. Though he had been wearing a helmet, he had suffered a concussion. We could see lacerations around his face and head from the impact of the crash. We were told that all of the ribs on his left side were broken. The bicycle handlebar had gone through his side and into the lining of his stomach. For the next few days, Andy was on painkillers and barely woke up. When medical aides shifted him, his shoulder dropped from his collarbone. He was taken back into surgery and the collarbone was bolted back together.

A friend from work at Wittenberg University knew a Lutheran minister in Knoxville who came to the hospital to pray with us. Andy was emotionally overwhelmed and sobbed. We felt God's presence. We thanked Him for saving Andy's life and asked for healing. To this day, I am reminded of the accident when I see the scar from Andy's belly button around his side to his spine. His left arm and hand still dangle limply.

After a week, BSS wanted to take Andy back to Ohio, but the doctors recommended against it. Despite their advice, BSS put Andy in his spacious flatbed pickup truck and drove him back to his home in Cuyahoga Falls, Ohio, where he spent one year convalescing. He didn't return to work until his physical therapy was finished. During that time the lawyer's card stayed in my purse. I couldn't possibly put my son through more trauma.

CHAPTER 13

Wittenberg University

After teaching for twelve years at Trinity Lutheran School in Cuyahoga Falls, Ohio, I resigned. The church had hired a new minister who did not support the school or the teachers. When I asked him why he didn't send his children to the Christian school, he said they were not sacrificial lambs. If he felt that way, his parishioners would not be sending their children to the school either. If the shepherd doesn't lead the sheep won't follow. Enrollment declined rapidly. Nine teachers, including me, found positions in other schools. I became a public-school substitute teacher until I could decide on a future career.

I dabbled in real estate, passing the Ohio real estate board test and working with a brokerage in an upper-middle-class community. I was rather naïve and did not understand the business world. When a client called to see a house, I would say, "Why don't you drive by and see if you like it? If so, I will take you inside." The other Realtors would laugh at me, saying, "You'll never make a sale. You have to get them in your car with their checkbooks in hand and drive them to the site." So that's why I never sold a house! I did sell my home and earned a $3,000 commission. Then I got BSS in my little red sports car with his checkbook and sold him our new condo in Springfield for another $3,000 commission. At least I earned some money in six months.

Before the move to Springfield, Ohio, I became ill with pneumonia for the third time. This time I had double pneumonia. After six months, I couldn't regain my strength, and moving to Springfield became very difficult. It was a good thing I wasn't working, but that didn't last long. Polly, a girlfriend from church, who was working at Wittenberg University, told me the university was looking for teachers to help start an accelerated experiential adult learning program. I applied for the position and was called in for an interview.

The interviewer, Dr. Webster, remembered my brother Ted, the missionary, and he also knew my father as the founder of the Cleveland Lutheran high schools. I had excellent credentials on my own. I provided my résumé, which documented my twelve years of teaching elementary school and showed that a Lutheran publishing company had printed my work on preschool and kindergarten learning units. I was hired!

The adult learning program was designed for students who had completed the first two years of college or sixty credits. Most of the students had gone directly from high school to college only to find they could not pass the courses. They dropped out of college to find employment. After twenty years of going nowhere on the job, they signed up to return to college for their undergraduate degrees. By this time, they were in their forties and ready to learn. The college offered three programs: health care, criminal justice, and business administration. There were ten seminars, each of which lasted six weeks.

At the beginning of the program, my job was to assign students to write their autobiographies. This was done for two reasons. First, I would assess students' writing skills for college-level abilities, and second, I would search for life experiences that might provide topics for research papers that could earn them three college credits. For example, a student who had suffered cancer could research the topic using five resources, describe his or her experience, and earn credits. I would check a research paper for grammatical errors before submitting it to the appropriate professor, who evaluated the learning content and awarded anywhere from zero to three credits.

Students also had the option of submitting professional school and training certificates that could also generate college credits. At their places of employment, many working people were offered courses such as computer training, the Evelyn Wood reading course, Dale Carnegie's course "The Power of Positive Thinking," and real estate licensing classes. I would study the course content and compare it to similar courses offered at local colleges. If they matched, I would give a student the same number of credits that a college course provided. This explains why the program was called "accelerated."

I aspired to teach the second of ten seminars, titled "Experiential Learning and Critical Thinking." This seminar was designed to give students the time management skills to coordinate work, college, and family life. I would teach students job search skills such as résumé writing, interview techniques, and etiquette. Students were also tested for personality type with the Meyers-Briggs Inventory and with the Learning Styles Inventory, which tested their ability to work with other styles. Unfortunately, I needed a master's degree in education to teach at the undergraduate level, and legally I could not use inventories without a degree in guidance and counseling with a focus on college student personnel.

The college financed my two-year program for a master's degree in guidance and counseling of college student personnel. I completed the program in one and a half years and graduated cum laude.

Wittenberg University was located in Springfield but the

college had several off-site campuses. I would travel around metropolitan Columbus, Ohio, to teach students at businesses such as automobile assembly plants and hospitals. On many a night, I wouldn't return to the main campus until midnight, especially when it snowed. When I drove the company car, Alex would come from home and dig my car out of the snow at the campus parking lot. When I drove directly home, he would be waiting for me in the driveway. What a wonderful guardian angel I had!

When teaching at a college it is important to keep upgrading your degree. I aspired to receive a doctorate. At that level, a student must be published. Since I had already accomplished that, I was well on my way toward a doctorate. That dream would never be possible when BSS told me he was retiring and we were moving to Florida.

CHAPTER 14

Where Is God?

We advised Alex to apply for admission to Columbus University upon graduation from high school. At least he could get two years of basic classes and then decide on a major field of study or enter a technical school for training. The college was close to home, but we encouraged him to get a taste of dormitory life. Besides, his best friend was going to Columbus University and wanted Alex to be his roommate. Alex didn't say it but I knew he was worried about his dad's behavior toward me. He had good reason to be concerned.

On Wednesday nights, BSS and I attended the free Wittenberg University orchestra performances at Luther Auditorium. We moved to Springfield because the city offered large libraries, bus services, concerts, theaters, hospitals, and health care facilities, all of which would be beneficial in our senior years.

One snowy Wednesday evening, we headed out to Luther Auditorium for a 7:00 p.m. performance. We didn't dress for the weather because we knew we could park next to the auditorium. Three cars were in line ahead of us in the street outside the parking facility. Without a word, BSS put the car in park, hopped out, and walked down the street. It was snowing quite heavily, and I couldn't see where he was headed. I moved into the driver's seat, drove down the block, and tried to spot him on the sidewalk. No luck, so I pulled into a metered parking lot on the street across from the auditorium. I guessed BSS had gotten impatient waiting for a parking spot and had walked over. I searched the lobby and the auditorium but couldn't find him.

My next option was to search the main street bars and convenience stores. The snow was coming down in sheets and I couldn't leave this man out in the cold. What should I do now? I reminisced about another time he had gone missing. We went to Springfield for a summer art fair on the city streets. Since I was eight months pregnant, BSS dropped Andy and me off at a corner while he parked the car. We waited there for three hours. Where was he? We walked to the police station on the next block. I asked officers to search for my husband. I learned that he had to be missing for twenty-four hours before he could be declared a missing person.

I knew I could not ask the police to help this time. At 11:00 p.m., I drove home in the cold, snowy night. BSS wasn't there. I stayed awake, waiting for the phone to ring. At 5:00 a.m. he walked into the house, covered from top to bottom with mud and snow. He didn't say a word, threw his muddy clothes in the washing machine, changed, and left the house. I didn't see him till spring. I guessed he had spent the past ten hours walking the five miles home.

In the summer, Alex was home from college and his dad was back from the boat. BSS bought a used two-seat Austin-Healy convertible kit car. It wasn't good for transportation, just fun in the sun. We used the car for just that purpose one sunny summer afternoon. Alex drove down Springfield's main street with me in the passenger seat and his dad crunched between us over the trunk. It wasn't long before BSS jumped out of the car and into the outdoor café bars. It took a while to find him. This was not a good scene for Alex to witness.

We took BSS home and put him to bed. Alex and I planned to go to the liquor cabinet and pour out the contents into the kitchen sink. BSS came downstairs and caught us in the act. He held his hands under the liquor and kept scooping it into his mouth.

After years of denigration, I never believed he would physically abuse me, but I was about to experience the worst night of my life. I could never tell the story until now. I'm coming forward to warn other men and women about the initial stages of abuse. If you are abused in any way, chances are a bridge has been crossed and the abuse will happen again with greater consequences. If you don't speak up, defend yourself, or seek help, the abuse will accelerate. It won't end.

If alcohol is involved, offenders should be told when it is altering their behavior. BSS would do things I never thought he was capable of thinking, let alone doing. Drinking brings out an inner personality just waiting to show its ugly face. The same goes for unfaithful behavior. If your mate has a wandering eye, it's best to clear the air right away or infidelity may happen again. Lastly, don't believe the offender when he says everything is your fault. That's a sure way to break you down, not to build you up.

One evening, BSS must have had enough to drink to show his rage toward me. Where did this rage come from? Sometimes you can't see the forest for the trees. In other words, if you're too close to the problem you need to step back to get the total picture. Friends could do that for me. They explained to me that his rage came from losing control of me. With each step of my career he hated me more.

Did BSS have that in mind when he came after me in the kitchen? I was standing in front of the sink when he attacked me from behind, kicking me about ten times. The jolt threw my head into the upper kitchen cabinets, causing my lips to swell and bleed. I needed safety. I ran to the adjoining bathroom and locked the door. Safe? No! He picked the lock and threw open the door. I ran for the phone to call 911. He ripped the phone out of the wall. He kicked in the pantry door, causing it to fall to the floor. BSS was losing strength when he tried to put it back up. He couldn't figure out what he'd done. I could see he was about ready to pass out, so I said, "I'm so tired and I see you're tired too. Let's go to bed and sleep it off." He fell into bed. I hid in a basement corner and found paper bags to write down the things that had happened that night. I was so traumatized I feared I would erase this event from my mind. I needed to document the abuse in case I was seriously injured or was found dead.

I talked to God a long time that night. "Where are You, God?" I asked. "In the past I trusted You would protect me. I watched and waited. I knew You loved me. For goodness' sake, You sent Your only Son to die on the cross for my sins. If You did that, You would not leave me in my darkest hour. God, I felt Your presence. The more I suffered, the closer I was to You. Through suffering You have given me perseverance. I honor You above all, and You have built character in my heart to love my neighbor as myself. You have given me hope never to give up. You have given me endurance. In answer to my question, God, You were there with me."

In addition, I had to understand the reason I was dealing with this problem. God was revealing Himself to me through this pain. I had been horribly hurt by someone who had vowed to love me. Through this pain, God had made me a better person. Would I inflict such pain on someone I loved or on any human being? Would I belittle another person to his or her face? No, not after I knew how it felt to be treated with disdain. Would I help another person experiencing abuse? Absolutely. That is why I am telling my story. God would never betray me. God would never leave me. He is my strength in trouble, and trouble was what I had.

Without forty years of abuse, I wouldn't have the slice of heaven I have now. The abuse, especially after that fateful night, led me to trust in God very deeply. I also trusted in ministers who interpreted the Bible correctly and not in BSS, who used the Bible to frighten me into submission. He knew I was not happy in our marriage, and he suspected I wanted a divorce, so he cunningly used the Bible to convince me that I would go to hell if I divorced him. He said, "God does not condone divorce. If you break your wedding vow you will go to hell."

BSS frightened me so badly that I told three ministers about his abuse and about my fear of breaking God's rules. The ministers assured me that God would not want me to live with an abusive man any longer. They also pointed out that it was my husband who had broken his wedding vow to love and to care for me till death do us part. Without intervention in this marriage, nothing would change.

That night, my thoughts turned to the people who cared for me. My brother and friend Ernest provided help. He would pop over to my house and hang around, and he saw for himself what I could not tell anyone. BSS mixed alcohol with anger and created violence. One night, he kicked over a glass table and threw Andy out of the house. Ernest spent several nights with me till morning came, and he saw BSS emerge as a different person who didn't remember what had happened the night before.

My son Alex was my best friend and helper. He knew the challenges I faced, and he didn't want to leave me alone with his dad. He decided to live at home instead of in the college dormitory and to commute to school.

My three best girlfriends—Polly, Sally, and Jean—encouraged me to pursue a divorce. They agreed with the Lutheran ministers and with the counselors that the marriage couldn't be saved. I pulled the lawyer's business card out of my purse and made an appointment. Her first question was, "What's going on?" I didn't know where to begin. She wasn't interested in hearing about my past, only about the current abuse.

Her next question was about careers and finances. I knew very little about my economic situation except that it always seemed we didn't have any money. When I told her about our careers, she questioned our supposed lack of income and asked why I didn't think I could survive on my own despite the fact that I had a master's degree in education. I couldn't think of an answer. BSS told me something different from reality.

What role did the Devil play in this mess? What part does he have in human misfortune? He tempts us to do what we don't want to do. As St. Paul observed so profoundly in Romans 7:14, "I don't really understand myself, for I want to do what is right, but I don't do it. I do what I hate." We struggle with sin. The Devil works extra hard to win Christians away from Jesus. He thinks that if he causes us to suffer enough we will not trust God. The opposite is true. When I suffer, I reach out for God's guiding hand, not the Devil's.

The Devil even had the nerve to tempt Jesus to win Him over to his side. Matthew 4:8 tells us that the Devil took Jesus to a high mountain and showed Him all the kingdoms of the world and their splendor. The Devil said, "All this I will give you if you bow down and worship me." Jesus said, "Away from me, Satan! For it is written, worship the Lord your God, and serve Him only." The Devil tempted Jesus three times in the desert, and Jesus won these battles. We can learn from Him. If we do what Jesus would do, we can keep the Devil at bay.

I humorously called my ex-husband the Beloved Son of Satan because it appeared the Devil tempted him with liquor and he did not resist. He had a black thundercloud hanging over his head, and the drizzle it produced led to my troubles with him. I still struggle with bitterness over our forty-year marriage. Then I remember to do what Jesus would do.

I told Andy about my intention to divorce his dad. Soon after, a very concerned Andy appeared at my door. He told me, "Mom, you will be unable to survive financially on your income." He was right. My yearly income at Wittenberg University was less than $30,000. I explained this to my lawyer, and she begged me not to abandon my efforts to get a divorce. She said I desperately needed to get out of the marriage. She emphasized her concern by telling me it was okay if I didn't want to hire her but I should get another lawyer.

Then I got the shock of my life. Apparently, BSS heard that I was seeing a lawyer. Your immediate thought would be that he grabbed another beer and passed out. Instead, he promised to stop drinking! I had never seen him practice sobriety, so could I trust that he would become and remain sober? Probably not. Should I support him in his efforts? He wanted us to start a new life together. Should I forgive the past?

Why is it so hard to forgive unconditionally? As a Christian, I believe the ultimate expression of forgiveness is God sacrificing His Son so our sins are forgiven. Because I have been forgiven, I should be forgiving. Forgiveness is difficult if the person who is sinning does not change his behavior, but if that person acknowledges the sin and makes an effort to change, forgiveness is necessary. What would Jesus do? I forgave.

John 8:3–11 tells how teachers of the law brought a woman caught in adultery to a group of people who gathered around Jesus. They told Jesus she must be stoned, but Jesus said, "If any one of you is without sin, let him be the first to cast a stone at her."

The people began to go away. Jesus said to the woman, "Where are they? Has no one condemned you?"

"No one," she said.

Jesus said, "Then neither do I condemn you. Go now and leave your life of sin."

CHAPTER 15

Moms Like to Say Good-bye

Mom retired at sixty-eight after selling her ornamental iron business to her accountant. Her mental health declined rapidly over the next ten years due to dementia. She would ask me if I had any children, a silly question since she frequently babysat both of my boys. She would ask me if she had ever been to my house. This disturbed me because at least once a week she would drive over for dinner. I would wave to her from my front yard as she drove off and would watch her narrowly avoid sideswiping parked cars.

I meant to talk to Mom about her ability to drive, but it was a hard topic to bring up. I didn't want her to lose her independence, but I knew it was time for her to stop driving. She realized this after she made a left turn into oncoming traffic. Her arm got stuck in the steering wheel and was severely cut and bruised. She and the car were in the bump shop for several weeks. Now I had a plan. Ted had four teenage boys and needed a second car, so I suggested that she give her car to him. That was okay with her as long as she gave all her other children cars too. Her generosity far surpassed her mental ability.

Now I had the responsibility of driving Mom where she wanted to go. She once called and asked me to take her to the beauty salon. I said, "I can't now but maybe later." About an hour later, I got a call from the salon. She wanted me to pick her up. I asked how she got there. She had called a taxi.

Grocery shopping was a challenge. Mom got so confused that it was difficult for her to select products. It was just a matter of time before she was unable to leave the house. She could not find her own front door. Ernest and I hired a home nursing service for weekdays, but she needed twenty-four-hour-a-day care. We knew she wanted to go to the Medina Lutheran Home where her relatives had been. We first had her stay weekdays at the nursing home and brought her back to her condo on weekends. That worked for a short time until she couldn't remember her home anymore.

Mom's dementia increased to the point where she was kept in a locked corridor to prevent her from leaving the nursing facility. She had a reputation for unknowingly misbehaving. At Christmastime, two nurses noticed ornaments were missing from a tree. They were sure Helen was the thief.

When Mom could no longer walk or talk, she was given a private room. I saw her every weekend or during the week when I wasn't teaching school. She could say only my name and "I love you." She could see me if she was wearing her glasses, but I was not sure if she could hear me. She would smile and nod her head to look like she could. I had conferences with doctors, social workers, dietitians, and nurses concerning her physical, social, physiological, and emotional welfare. Mom's needs were small. She liked the knee-high nylons and fleecy sweat suits that I bought her regularly. She couldn't tell me but I knew she loved chocolate bars, so I always brought one when I came. She would hum for more.

One Sunday morning in September as my mother neared her ninety-second birthday, the front desk nurse called and said, "Your mom will not live through the day. You better come right away if you want to say good-bye." I relayed the information to BSS. Drunk or sober his response was always the same: "Nobody's telling me what I'm going to do. I'm not rushing down there." I replied, "That's fine, but I'm leaving now." He relented and got in the car with me. I took my Lutheran hymnal to sing Mom's favorite songs and to say prayers.

Entering her room, I found Mom lying in bed on her side with her eyes wide open. I knew right away she knew me. She couldn't say "I love you, Maggie," but I saw it in her eyes. She was covered with a sheet, but I could see parts of her hands. They were as black as coal and so were her arms. I lifted the sheet and saw that her legs and feet were also black. Her heart was working hard to keep her brain and vital organs alive.

For several hours, I sang the hymns and prayed the prayers I knew Mom could remember. I could tell by looking into her eyes that she heard me. About noon, I told her I was going across the street to grab a hamburger at McDonald's. In the car, BSS said he wanted to check on our boat in dry storage a few miles down the street. I protested but he did it anyway. Then we stopped at McDonald's. I sat at a table, looked across the street, and saw a black hearse approaching the front door of the nursing home. I ran out the door, entered the home, and saw Mom's covered body being wheeled out on a gurney. The nurse said that Mom had died just after I left but that I shouldn't feel guilty, because it was common for dying people to know when their loved ones exited the room and to take the opportunity to pass away.

Relatives and friends came from faraway places to say good-bye to Mom. My loving and caring coworkers from Wittenberg University came in a van to pay their respects. The funeral was on a Wednesday. I had previously asked my in-laws to come over for brunch on Saturday. Despite my exhaustion and unhappiness, I kept the engagement. When my in-laws appeared at my front door, my mother-in-law offered her usual greeting, saying, "You look haggard."

"Of course I do," I responded. "My mother died and was buried this week." When she replied bitterly that her mother had also died, I told her, "Your mother died when you were two years old. You don't even remember your mother." It was quite obvious who had taught BSS how to get along with people.

BSS's mother proved to be the downfall of her son. She would control people by threatening, "If you don't do as I say, I will stop eating or maybe even never talk to you again." How many times did I hear BSS say the same things to me? His favorite comment was, "If you would change, I would stop drinking." His mom's threats got serious when she stopped eating and had to be hospitalized. She would violently pull out her IVs, jump out of bed, and try to escape from the hospital. That's how she lost a front tooth. She was put in a straitjacket so she wouldn't hurt herself or others. Her husband and daughter tried to feed her, but she would not respond.

She was transferred to a nursing home. When she saw me enter her room she screamed, "Maggie, please help me." Though she had used and abused me since I met her, I forgave her and said, "What can I do to help you?" Her feet were cold. She wanted her socks from her dresser at home. I promised to bring them the next day.

Searching through her drawers, I couldn't miss the socks because there must have been fifty pairs. That seemed strange. Doing more research, I discovered she had obsessions with items such as tomato soup. She had stocked more cans than I could count. Her greeting card collection could have filled a Hallmark shop. When she learned how to crochet, she couldn't stop making blankets. I was the proud recipient of many of them. And those pictures of fruit mounted on pieces of wood were all over my house. She loved candy, so what did she give up for Lent? I caught her eating peanut M&Ms a week before Easter. She told me they weren't candy but peanuts.

The next day, I returned to the nursing home with her socks. She had a food tray positioned over her bed. She was refusing food from her family. Incredibly, she ate for me. Whom was she trying to control, if anyone? It seemed to me, as an outsider, that her family was the target. It wasn't long before she died of starvation. She did it to herself. At her funeral, her friends showed her no mercy. They looked at her and told me she got what she wanted.

CHAPTER 16

A Boat Named Steadfast

Sobriety wasn't what I thought it would be, though I wasn't expecting perfection. The underlying mental problems that BSS had twice admitted were evident. He looked gaunt, wide-eyed, and tired. He seemed nervous, apprehensive, and very unsure of himself. I associated his trembling with withdrawal from alcohol. Since this might be a temporary condition, I was patient.

For the first time BSS told me he was sorry, though his apology came in strange circumstances. We were traveling in our blue Buick SUV from Birmingham, Alabama, where Andy lived with his family, to our Florida residence. I suffered from hip and back arthritis, so I stretched out in the rear of the car where there was plenty of room. We were headed south on I-75 in Florida when BSS stopped at a rest area and got out of the car. I decided to stretch by walking the trash up to the bathroom area. I was gazing at the beautiful countryside from a hill overlooking the highway when suddenly I saw our SUV entering I-75 south. There I was, stranded at a rest area without money or a purse.

Truck drivers approached me and asked if I was lost. "Oh no," I said. "I just enjoy reading road maps here in the rest area." I wondered how long it would take BSS to realize I wasn't in the car. Knowing him, he might drive all the way home without me. I found a pay phone, dialed 911, and told the operator my husband had left me at a rest area. She laughed and asked, "Did he leave you there on purpose?"

"No," I replied. "He's just going through a hard time and he's not very observant. I need a state trooper to look for a blue Buick SUV on I-75 south."

So the wait began. I didn't have my watch, but I surmised a few hours went by and still no Buick. Maybe BSS did leave me there on purpose.

Eventually, the Buick reappeared at the entrance to the rest area. BSS said he was sorry but he traveled twenty miles before noticing I was not in the car. Why did it take him so long to return? He explained that when he turned around to come back north, he saw the rest area on I-75 south after twenty miles, but there were no northbound exits for miles since this was a rural area. It was almost evening by the time he headed south. Here's the message. Don't leave anyone or anything behind at a rest area. By the way, the state trooper never found him. Was life better now that BSS was sober?

Many more changes were to come in this new life together. At fifty-two, BSS told me he was retiring within the year. At forty-eight, I did not have retirement in my plans. I wanted to continue teaching at Wittenberg University and to work on my doctorate in education compliments of the college. But I had to agree with his decision to retire. I didn't think he could stand the pressure of his financial analyst position at General Motors any longer.

Here's the bait BSS dangled in front of me to get me to retire. He would purchase the boat I fell in love with nine years earlier. Back in the summer of 1988, we were sailing our thirty-four-foot boat by the Tartan sailboat factory on the Grand River in Ohio and observed a forty-foot navy blue sailboat being transported down to the river for a test run. I commented that it was the most beautiful sailboat I'd ever seen.

It was being built for our friends from Sandusky Marina. Tim was an executive with Goodyear Tire Company, and Betty was a nurse at Christ Hospital. These occupations did not prepare them for the difficulties of sailing a boat. The boat was a sloop, so it had one main mast with a sail rising forty-five feet above sea level. Consequently Tim and Betty traveled from port to port by turning on the diesel engine. They owned the boat about two years without sailing it. They lost interest, but more significantly they lost interest in each other. The boat was put in dry dock and up for sale. We were semi-interested in purchasing the boat if the price was right. BSS called Tim one evening and made him a low-ball offer. Tim said he was drunk but not that drunk.

A few years later, a doctor bought the sailboat and put it in a slip at the marina. Soon after, he was diagnosed with bone cancer and was unable to operate the boat. He could do only minor maintenance. When he passed away, the boat was back in dry storage for four years. We again inquired about the boat and discovered that two couples had agreed to buy it. However, only one couple was approved for financing. After nine years, the boat had never been sailed, and the time and the price were right for us.

Now that we were both retired, we prepared the boat for a long journey from Ohio to Florida. Using my sewing skills, I upholstered the v-berth and settee cushions and made pillows and sail covers. We purchased and studied charts for months. In May, we were ready to leave our dock, but we had to wait for gale-force winds and ten-foot seas to subside. Eventually, we crossed Lake Erie from the west to the east in calm seas. At the entrance to the Erie Canal, our forty-five-foot mast had to be taken down and laid on the cabin top because the canal had several low bridges that would otherwise be impassable.

We prepared for our journey through the canal's twenty-eight locks. We had to tap the engine cylinder to get the boat's start button to work. This problem had occurred several times before, but this time it created a fire. The fire spread from the cabin to the start button in the cockpit. BSS stared in shock. I entered the cabin, which was full of smoke, and put out the fire with an extinguisher. The boat would be inoperable until an electrician rewired the cable. The people at the marina where we were staying could not recommend anyone. A group of people were picnicking and drinking beer in a park near the dock. A man told us he was an electrician and would take a look at the damage. Four hours later, the boat was fixed better than before, or so we hoped.

After the fire, the captain and his first mate were not psychologically ready for the upcoming adventure. I wish we could have predicted the future, because we would have turned around. Seeing the first of the locks was overwhelming. We didn't know what to expect. The massive lock doors opened and we saw large cement walls. Some boaters used bales of hay for bumpers between their boats and the walls. We put out our rubber fenders, which worked just as well and left no mess. We had lines on the bow and stern reaching to the cleats on the walls. Since I recently had finger surgery and needed surgery on other fingers, it was difficult for me to handle the lines, so I became the captain. The role reversal was also important since the previous captain was despondent over the boat's condition.

The next lock appeared in less than thirty minutes, followed by another and another. There was no time to relax. Further down the canal, a lock was situated next to a thirty-foot waterfall, making it difficult to enter. The river current pulled the boat toward the falls. I circled around and around, waiting for the lock to open. I took a deep breath when the massive doors swung open and the boat slipped past the falls.

To our surprise, we entered a large lake about midway through the canal. Here our four-and-a-half-foot stationary keel with a retractable six-foot keel dropped to a depth of ten and a half feet. The line holding it in place had broken. We had to raise the keel because the canal in most places was only nine feet deep. Think! Think! How could we do this without the attached line?

We found a long rope, went to the bow, and walked the rope on each side under the haul until it was beneath the keel. We attached each end of the rope to wenches on each side of the boat. We cranked the wenches until the retractable keel was lifted and tied the ends of the rope on top of the cabin. The rope looked like a bow on a birthday present. Would it hold? God only knew, but at least we were okay for the time being.

Then we noticed our diesel supply diminishing. Why were there no gas stations along the canal for boaters? At the fourteenth lock we found a dilapidated dock with diesel hoses lying on the ground. We had our tank filled, but could there be dirt in the diesel fuel? We had to trust in God that the fuel was clean.

The terrain between the locks was interesting. The canal was built of concrete and in many places was much higher than the land level. At the east end, the Erie Canal connected to the Hudson River. We stopped in Albany, New York, to rest overnight. Heading south the next morning, we were shocked to see the massive Federal Lock, which was the width of the river. Inside, a freighter was tied to the left concrete wall. We entered the doors where the water was churned up by winds and current. It was difficult to tie lines to the right concrete wall without smashing the boat.

The front lock doors didn't open for at least an hour. Hanging on to the bow lines was tedious. I prayed to God to help me hold on just a little bit longer. When the doors opened, I changed my mind and prayed, "Please don't let me out in that river!" The waves were high and the current was swift. The mast was tied to the top of the cabin, and the wind threatened to roll it into the heavy seas. We had to turn right to enter a river that would lead us to Riverside Marina where our mast was to be lifted back into place. Channel markers at the turn guided us to the deep-water entrance.

BSS did not stay within the marks because turning the boat sideways to the waves might have thrown the mast overboard. He came wide into the channel, landing us on a sandbar where the water was two feet deep. In the low tide the boat started to roll over on its side. I rushed into the cabin to take the dishes out of the cupboards and to put away loose items. We abandoned ship and rode our vinyl dinghy to shore.

For four hours we waited and watched for the nine-foot tide to flow back into the river and raise the boat. Then we rode the dinghy back to the boat in the dark. We put the boat in a dock. The captain was done. He called a freighting company to haul the boat to Tampa Bay, Florida.

Canceling the adventure broke my heart. I almost had the chance to sail by the Statue of Liberty and into the Atlantic Ocean, but I could not do that alone. The captain lost twenty pounds and looked frail. He couldn't go on. I was kidding myself if I believed his depression was temporary. The experience drove him to mental instability, I found out later. I suffered physically. My hands took a beating handling the boat lines. I tried to pamper the finger on which the knuckle had been replaced with a screw. Now other fingers needed bone removal, and the balls in my wrist sockets had been dislodged.

Despite the misadventures, I thanked God for bringing us back to land. His presence in my life was more evident each day. What better name than *Steadfast* for the boat that took us safely hundreds of miles and remained strong?

CHAPTER 17

Time to Rethink

We finally met up with *Steadfast* at the Regatta Pointe Marina on the Bradenton River flowing out of the Gulf of Mexico in Tampa, Florida. The marina accommodated many live-aboard boaters, and we stayed on our boat until BSS decided to buy a house in Florida and not to return to Ohio. I called the captain a land lover. Clearly, we wouldn't be taking a boat trip soon.

With the arthritis worsening in my hands and in other parts of my body, I was glad to stay away from the cold northern weather and to enjoy the hot southern sunshine, which soothed my joints. My hand surgeon in Ohio recommended I see Dr. Painless, a hand surgeon in Tampa. Thus began a series of four surgeries involving the removal of my fingers' first knuckles and their replacement with hinges. In addition, the balls in both of my wrist sockets had to be reinserted. It was a slow process because, for obvious reasons, only one hand could be operated on at a time.

Between surgeries, I pursued my career in education. I attended a Lutheran church in Bradenton that had a preschool-through-second grade program. I read in the church bulletin that the school was hiring a principal, and I made an appointment for an interview. As I approached the front door, I looked in to see one of the preschool classes line up to go outside for recess. The children were poorly supervised and were hitting and kicking each other. The teachers, dressed in T-shirts and cutoff shorts, were yelling for order. I saw that the school needed structure. Providing that would be a challenge but I was ready for it. I was hired the next day and on the job.

And what was the job? I was told to go buy juice and crackers for the next week's snacks. My other responsibility was to speak with disgruntled parents who were upset because other children were hitting their child. The second-grade teacher was in charge of all the bills and purchases. The board of education hired and fired teachers. I learned that I was the fourth principle hired that year. The board members didn't want me to have control, but they needed my master's degree in education to keep the school open. I thought I could make a difference, but that's not what they wanted. I was employed there for three months.

Still desiring a position in education, I inquired at the Manatee County public school system about its adult education program. Its business and industry division hired me to teach a course I developed called "Getting Along in the Workplace" at large local businesses that promoted employee training. It was rewarding work but the presentations were few and far between. Southwest Florida had very few businesses that sponsored employee training programs.

Coming home from work wasn't easy. I would find BSS in the same leather chair he was in when I left in the morning. He seldom went anywhere except to the library to check out seven or eight books, usually about the Civil War. He seldom took care of *Steadfast*. I believed his depression was deepening, but I couldn't even suggest that to him. He said I was the problem, and he became more despondent and withdrawn. Little did I know that our life would soon change.

CHAPTER 18

Deadly Accidents

Between seeking school positions, I was back in Tampa General Hospital for my third hand surgery. This time the ball in my right wrist had to be put back into the socket, and two fingers needed hinges to replace the arthritic knuckles. Since I am right-handed, I was disabled for six weeks.

That wasn't all bad. At least I got the couch potato off of his chair and into the grocery store to help me. He grabbed a bottle of white wine and put it in the shopping cart. He said it was for me though five years earlier, when he promised to stop drinking, I committed to join him so I wouldn't tempt him with liquor in the house. Because he bought my favorite white wine instead of beer or hard liquor, I suspected he would blame me if he started drinking again.

When BSS cracked open that bottle our lives changed forever. I should have known the repercussions of that first drink, but I didn't want to overreact. I didn't know the future and never would have guessed that my life could become a slice of heaven. God had a plan for my life although it's hard to see that when things go wrong. When the good times come, they are greatly appreciated.

By this time, I was nearing my mid-fifties and was a ball of energy. I heard a television report that the new University of South Florida was being built in Tampa. Management was looking for staff and teachers from all over the United States. I was fortunate to be hired in student services to establish a career development center. This involved setting up a resource library, contacting local businesses about student job placement and internship programs, conducting job searches on the Internet, and counseling graduating seniors for job placement. The process started with writing a résumé and learning interview skills and follow-up techniques. It was very gratifying to be in the helping profession.

One year after creating the career development center, I was beginning to turn over many of the responsibilities to student help. Sitting at my desk one morning, I received a phone call from Broward Community College, also in Tampa. The provost had heard about my reputation for creating programs in Ohio and Florida. He wanted to set up a continuing adult education program on his Manatee County campus and asked me when I could come in for an interview.

There were lots of positives to consider. The campus was located just a short distance from my home. The salary was much higher than I'd ever earned before. Most of all, the challenge was exciting. I gave the University of South Florida two weeks' notice and began a new career. In the first year, I increased a seven-class program to seventy-five classes. I accomplished this by reading a book on marketing and following through with the process. The provost started me off by taking me to a Manatee Chamber of Commerce meeting at a golf and country club. He introduced me to members and handed out my business card while announcing that he was bowing out and giving me the responsibility.

I took the hint. I enrolled in similar community organizations to promote adult education in the community. I was the guest speaker at groups such as the Tampa University Women's Club, the Elks Club, a men's club called SCORE, and the American

Legion. Two radio stations were glad to have me as a guest speaker on their half-hour Sunday morning shows. Imagine my son's surprise when his radio went on one sleepy Sunday morning and he heard his mother's voice.

My greatest source of publicity was the article I wrote once a month for the *Tampa Bay Times* newspaper. By connecting community activities with course offerings, I encouraged readers to enroll in noncredit continuing education. For example, if an art fair was advertised in town, I would offer classes in art media to prepare people for the event. Most important, I developed brochures and took them up and down main streets, delivering them to restaurants, doctor's offices, and wherever else I was permitted to place them on counters.

My concerns were at home. It is difficult think about, let alone recount, how BSS started to drink again. He went from a silent depression to extreme highs and lows. I never knew what to expect. When I got up in the morning, the first thing he said to me was, "What is your problem?" When I came home in the evening, I would ask him what he did all day. He would say, "It's none of your business." I learned never to ask that question again.

I learned a lot more than that. I loved to cook, especially baking seven hundred cookies and pastries at Christmastime as gifts for family and friends. I soon found out that my five-course dinners were not appreciated. I would serve dinner to BSS, he would look it over, get up from his chair, go to the sink, and throw it down the disposal, commenting, "That's what I think of your meals."

"If you don't like the food," I told him, "don't dump it down the disposal. Save it in the refrigerator for my lunch. Also, you should cook what you like." That he did. His meals included hot dogs and hamburgers. One evening, he set his frying pan on the

Corian countertop and burned a circle in the top, causing the Corian to split. You'll learn more about this later.

BSS was not impressed with my domestic skills. My inclination to keep everything neat and clean must come from my German heritage, primarily my father, who kept his pink Cadillac polished and pristine. Whenever I spent time sweeping, dusting, and scrubbing the kitchen and the bathrooms, BSS would say, "If I wanted to sit around all day and watch someone clean, I would have married my mother." I couldn't help but think, *I wish you had.*

Every morning, I was off to Broward Community College. My downfall may have been accepting that position as head of the noncredit continuing education program. It was one of the five most respected and responsible jobs on campus. How did BSS feel about that? Was he proud? Was he thankful? Was he supportive? I believe we grew even further apart.

As I was driving to work on a small county road one morning, I looked at my bucket seat and saw Jesus. He asked me where I was headed so fast. I explained that I was sponsoring the Manatee County Chamber of Commerce breakfast meeting at Broward Community College that morning. Jesus told me I better slow down. Did I listen?

Next thing I knew, His angel, a state trooper, was right behind me flashing her lights. I pulled over to the soft shoulder and graciously received my speeding ticket. Oh no, my car would not start. I had a dead battery. Neither the state trooper nor I had jumper cables. She called another trooper to assist but he couldn't help either. I asked them if they could push the car to get it started, but legally they couldn't. I called BSS, asking him to bring jumper cables or to push the car. He must have been doing eighty when he pulled up. Too bad he wasn't under the radar. When BSS got out of the car, he approached the male trooper but never spoke to me. He must have been possessed by his dad, the Devil, because he was denigrating Broward Community College with the F-word.

I stood next to the woman trooper with tears flowing down my face like Niagara Falls. BSS never looked at me or said a word to me. He pushed my little red sports car and got it started. I drove off with my copilot. Sometimes bad things happen for good reasons. I was much more careful driving because I had a precious passenger in the other bucket seat.

More crazy things were going on. BSS was spending a lot of time reading on the boat instead of at home. He returned one evening and claimed that he found rat poison on the boat and that I was trying to kill him. If indeed he found rat poison, I didn't put it there but I wondered who did. When family pictures were taken, at the last minute BSS would hide behind the person in front of him, making himself invisible. Even worse, when family or friends were coming to our home for a visit he would disappear and suddenly reappear when they left. I was speechless.

Crazy things were also happening at church. Regardless of where I have lived, I have always been an active church member. Associating with people of the same religion has been a good way to make friends. We became members of a community Lutheran church where a group of people in their mid-fifties joined together for dinners and work projects.

In December, we were in charge of decorating the church for Christmas. We put two Christmas trees in the chancel and wreaths on the windows. That night, I made the mistake of wearing brand-new deck shoes. I was climbing up and down a twelve-foot ladder, decorating the tree with ornaments. My foot slipped on a rung and I fell to the floor. Two men in the back of the church ran to my rescue as BSS stood right next to me. He said I was an embarrassment and did not need help. Later that evening, the group met at a pizzeria. After looking through the menu, BSS slammed it down on the table and walked out the door. I looked at the stunned faces of sixteen people and said, "I guess I'm leaving."

My fear of being physically abused after the first incident years before in Ohio now became a reality. Our Florida home had one large bedroom with a queen-size bed. BSS counted the wooden posts on the headboard, found the middle one, and drew an imaginary line down the mattress. He told me I was not allowed to cross that line. Fine by me, except with my arthritic hips and back pain I would toss and turn unknowingly in the night. When I crossed that line, BSS would kick me unmercifully, leaving sores. I would blame myself for not following the rules. I believed I deserved to be punished.

My problem was recognizing abuse for what it was. I couldn't believe he would hurt me without cause. I didn't realize until years later that I had done nothing wrong. I don't believe anyone should be allowed to kick a dog let alone a person without intervention. An abused dog deserves a better home and so did I.

I was a busy lady but not too busy to take care of my health. I had yearly physical examinations. I never liked surprises but that year I had one. My white and red blood cell counts indicated cancer. My primary physician recommended a local cancer specialist. After several blood tests over the next three months, she said I had non-Hodgkins lymphoma or leukemia. She was mystified that I didn't show signs of fatigue.

The news was so startling to BSS that he decided to take a vacation to see relatives in Ohio. He boasted that it was the best vacation he ever had. So much for spousal support. While he was gone, I found comfort listening to tape recordings of brother Ted's church services. Hearing his voice and abiding by his words of encouragement brought me closer to trusting in God.

To verify the findings, the cancer specialist removed a piece of my hip bone and sent it to a New York laboratory. A few weeks later the report came back saying there was no cancer anywhere in my body. Only 5 percent of people could live with this blood cell count, and I was one of them. Was it God's idea to change a medical report in my favor? He definitely had a reason for me to stick around. I heard Him saying, "That's for Me to know and you to find out."

My life was saved, but my niece's life and her mother's were cut short. I always said my sister Wanda was born with a pickle in her mouth, which irritated her children, especially Carol. She and Wanda didn't see eye to eye. Although Carol excelled in high school, becoming the class valedictorian, she suffered from depression and antisocial behavior.

One Sunday, I asked Wanda if she would like to go to Bill Knapp's for lunch. To my delight, she invited her two daughters, Carol and Casey. I noticed Casey looked robust, so much better than her super-thin figure at eighteen years old when she was addicted to drugs. She eventually had to be hospitalized and taken to a rehabilitation center. The center's window washer entered her room, got her pregnant, and left her with the responsibility of raising the child. Casey must have done a pretty good job because the child went on to be a star college hockey player and a college graduate.

Carol seemed unsure of herself, almost jittery, although she spoke highly of her occupation as a lab technician. As always, I had filled my truck with clothes for Carol. She was my size and appreciated the clothes I couldn't use. Little did I know that she wouldn't need them. The next morning, she drove to Cincinnati, Ohio, and stopped at a high bridge over rapidly moving water. She left her car near the bridge with a suicide note that read, "Please don't let my mother near Casey's child." Her body was found further downstream and sent to a local funeral home in a body bag. When I told the story to BSS, he asked me what I had said to her at lunch. I didn't know if he was serious or trying to be funny. After her funeral, more information emerged about Carol's past. She had tried to commit suicide many times, unbeknown to me. She once drove up to northern Michigan in a snowstorm, left her car on the road, and tried to bury herself in a snow bank. The police found the car, searched the area, and dug her out. Back home, she had tried to hang herself, slit her wrists, and overdose on pills. She was caught every time.

I wish Carol had cried out for help. Maybe I wouldn't have had an answer, but I would have seen her more often and comforted her. Life changes. The problems of today can turn into joy in the morning. Don't ever give up. If Carol had known that her mother would die in six months, would she have committed suicide? I doubt it.

Wanda's life was cut short after her car was hit from behind by a careless driver one evening in Cleveland. The front of her car was thrown into a telephone pole. When the police arrived, they asked her if she was injured. She got out of the car and said no. Later that night, she fell into a coma and remained in it for ten days until she died.

For years, Wanda's children were concerned over her large stomach. She refused to see a doctor, but they knew something was wrong. After she died the children requested an autopsy. A cancerous stomach tumor about the size of a watermelon was discovered. I don't think she wanted to face the threat of cancer after seeing what our sister Annette went through. In His mercy, God took her to heaven suddenly.

Getting to Wanda's funeral on time was difficult. I managed to find a nonstop flight the night before the service. The plane was scheduled to land at Cleveland Hopkins Airport at 11:00 p.m.

the day before the funeral, but it was sidetracked. From Tampa, we flew to Fort Lauderdale, Florida, to pick up more passengers. These passengers had to be dropped off at Atlantic City, New Jersey, which put me at Cleveland Hopkins Airport at 4:30 a.m. Ernest had been waiting all night for my arrival. We got to the funeral just before Wanda's body was taken to the cemetery.

The trip home was uneventful until I got to Tampa International Airport where BSS was supposed to pick me up on concourse B. Arriving, I saw no trace of him. I waited almost an hour before taking the elevator to baggage claim. I had no baggage but maybe he didn't know that. Still no trace of him. I walked outside to the driveway, thinking he was waiting in the car by baggage pickup. No sign of him for four hours. Where had I seen this before? How many other times had he disappeared?

When BSS showed up he was screaming at me from one side of the airport to the other, causing a disturbance. I asked God to take away my anger, because my mind was saying over and over again, *I hate him.*

One month after my sister's fatal accident, I was heading to the college to give a speech to the Manatee County Economic Development Council. I was driving my little 2001 red convertible sports car with old-fashioned wire wheels that didn't adhere properly to the tires, a problem that had caused flats. I was a bit nervous and anxious to get to work. The speed limit on the small county road from my house was fifty-five mph. I was going sixty, so I wasn't out of control. The speed limit was probably too high for a road with two small lanes and no shoulders.

The side of the road was heavily potholed and full of muddy grass. My front right tire veered off the road into a pothole and went flat. Next the rear right tire went flat, causing the car to spin around backward at sixty mph. Thank goodness there was no traffic. The car crossed over the road, flew over a ditch, and chopped off a tree six feet up. I was conscious the whole time. I can't say I was thinking about God. I tried to control the car but I couldn't. I guess I was just hoping the car would stop.

My landing was disastrous. The front end of the car was embedded in dirt and grass. I couldn't see the rear end, so I assumed it was missing. I sat in my bucket seat examining my arms and legs. I had no bruises or cuts. I thought I must be looking down from heaven, because I had no injuries. In the seat next to me, I saw Jesus and I asked Him, "Jesus, why didn't You take the wheel?" Then I saw three men looking in my window. One of them said, "Don't move. An ambulance is coming." I said I felt fine. Then I remembered my sister's car accident the month before. She thought she was fine too.

I agreed to be removed from the car on a board and placed in an ambulance for a trip to the hospital. X-rays and an examination proved I was fine. From the hospital window I had seen my car being towed to a body shop. I went there to view the damage and was told I better look for a new car. I pleaded with the body mechanic to fix my special car with ground effects and other unusual features. Six-thousand dollars later it was fixed minus the wire wheels. Jesus liked riding with me in my little red convertible.

In the past, I had asked God where He was. I didn't do that now. He was in the passenger seat right next to me. As for the three men who approached my car, I didn't know where they came from. I didn't see another car. I believe they were God's angels taking care of me. Again, I asked God, "What are you saving me for?" He is answering me now when I feel a need to help other people experiencing pain, suffering, and the loss of loved ones.

I especially cared for my neighbor Teresa and she for me. Our life experiences were very similar. She had a great sense of humor despite having a rough marriage. She managed to get through tests for ovarian cancer with very little support from her husband, something I understood. I was with my sister when she died from ovarian cancer, so I knew what Teresa was going through. I couldn't see her driving to cancer treatment by herself, so I drove her there. I also took her out to lunch and for antique hunting.

After chemotherapy, Teresa didn't feel capable of driving to Tampa Airport to pick up friends, so I drove her car and picked them up. That was a blessing because when I saw how old her friends were, I realized they couldn't carry their luggage.

Little did I know what was happening back home while I was away. Upon my return, I found a police car in my driveway. I didn't know where BSS was, but apparently he had been there. A burglar, who was painting the exterior of my neighbor's house the day before, had attempted to rob my house and other neighbors' houses without success. He cut the screen on my lanai door, entered, and pried at the lock on the sliding door. He wasn't the sharpest pencil in the box, because he didn't try the other slider, which was unlocked.

A neighbor, sitting on his lanai smoking a cigarette, witnessed the break-in, chased the burglar off of my lanai, and called a security guard, who called the police. The security guard found BSS incoherent on the boat. After the excitement, I didn't feel safe, knowing a burglar was in the area.

The next day, when the coast was clear, BSS came home to blame me for the attempted break-in. He said the painter must have seen me Rollerblading around the community, followed me home, and later tried to assault me. If he believed that was true, why didn't he stay home that evening to protect me? BSS also knew the painter had attempted to enter two other houses before trying to break into ours, so why was he anxious to make me feel guilty?

In appreciation for my neighbor's efforts, the next day I gave him a whole carton of cigarettes. Little did I know that when he saw the burglar my neighbor was smoking his last cigarette. His wife did not appreciate my generosity.

My dear friend Teresa got better for a brief time. She laughed about her bald head and liked to show it off by not wearing her wig. She and her husband, Jack, had a party one evening and invited BSS and me as well as several other couples. Jack, a heavy drinker himself, filled BSS's glass once too often. I was sitting on a sofa on the lanai and looked over into the living room. There was BSS passed out on the floor. Embarrassed, I got him up and walking and said good-bye.

BSS got into the driver's seat of the car and tried to move the stick shift, but he kept rocking the car back and forth. I was afraid he would back up far enough to wind up in the river. I pleaded with him to get out of the driver's seat. I didn't think he could see or hear me. Finally, I slapped his face to wake him up. Still no response. I ran upstairs to Teresa's condo and asked the strongest man I could find to help me. He told BSS to get out of the driver's seat. I wondered why BSS wouldn't do that for me. The man drove us to the boat and stayed until BSS dozed off.

I found three grocery bags and packed up everything on the boat that belonged to me. At midnight, I walked a mile back home and promised myself that I would never be on the boat again. I was fearful that BSS would get in the house.

CHAPTER 19

Camelot Is Not Forever

Ted was blessed to live seven years after his pancreatic cancer diagnosis, but high body temperatures were sapping his strength. Ted and Vicky spent those years traveling and visiting her parents in Nebraska. They would fly from California to Nebraska and then rent a car to drive to Vicky's hometown. On their last trip Ted's temperature was accelerating. Vicky couldn't get the rental car's air conditioner to work, so she tried to roll down the windows. They didn't work either. Her last resort was to open the doors as she drove to the nearest hospital. She didn't make it in time. Ted was buried with Vicky's family in Nebraska.

A month later, Ernest and I flew to his funeral service in Sacramento, California. At least fifteen ministers from all over the country honored Ted with eulogies. I was proud to be his sister. I questioned why God took him to heaven and didn't leave him on earth to spread the gospel of saving grace. Vicky answered my question when she reminded me that had it not been for his pancreatic cancer Ted wouldn't have written letters in praise of God to Lutheran churches in America. He taught people how to die peacefully. He was God's messenger.

On the heels of Ted's passing, Russ, my eldest brother, was diagnosed with vertigo, which seemed to explain his imbalance on airplanes. When the trouble persisted, further tests revealed astrocytoma, a cancerous brain tumor. Dad had died of the same thing thirty years earlier, and recently my nephew had a benign brain tumor. While Russ was hospitalized for cancer he contracted pneumonia, the ultimate cause of death. Some of his ashes were buried in the family plots in Ohio, and the rest were spread over Lake of the Woods where he vacationed in the summer. Ernest and I attended both services. I guess BSS didn't think it was important to be at the funerals.

Yet another brother, Gary, was dealing with the death of his son. Oh, dear God, stop the bleeding. A son should not die before his mother and father do, but we suspected that would happen when Jeff was a young child. Gary and Patty had two girls, seven and eight years old, when Jeff was born. Ernest and I were there soon after the joyful occasion to help care for the girls. We returned every summer to visit Gary and Patty in their beautiful home and cottage on Lake Tahoe.

At around two years old, Jeff seemed withdrawn and sullen, not in the terrible twos mold. Ernest and I noticed he wasn't walking normally or talking plainly. When Jeff was in elementary school, his teachers told Gary and Patty that he was a slow learner. By high school, Jeff was having petite seizures and some grand mal seizures, and he needed to be medicated. The seizures increased in intensity and frequency.

One summer Sunday afternoon, several people were having a picnic at Gary's home on the lake. It was great fun to jump into the four feet of water from a nearby dock. Amid all of the beach and water activities, someone noticed that Jeff was missing. A young guy looked down from the dock and spotted Jeff under the water, not breathing. He brought him to shore, gave him CPR, and restored air to his lungs. It was determined that Jeff fell off the dock while having a seizure. He was immediately hospitalized, but he had spent too much time underwater and had suffered brain damage.   .

Jeff was unable to live alone or even with his parents. He was institutionalized and later lived in a supervised group home. He was able to work in a garden nursery watering flowers but couldn't do much more. Gary and Patty would occasionally bring him back to their lake home for a weekend. On one such weekend, Gary and Patty woke up at eight Sunday morning and couldn't find Jeff. They walked down to the dock and discovered him floating in the lake. They surmised he had woken up early, taken a walk to the dock, and had another grand mal seizure. He was found too late to be saved.

Alex and I attended the funeral. I guess BSS had more important things to do than to mourn. I couldn't imagine the pain Gary and Patty were enduring in losing a twenty-nine-year-old son. Little did I know that Alex would also die at twenty-nine. Sometimes our plans aren't the same as God's plan, but in His mercy, He knows what is best for us.

Camelot was not forever and neither was Gary. He lost his fight for life as I was finishing this book. He stayed strong to be with Patty in the final stages of her Parkinson's disease. She died a year ago, and he missed her deeply. He was eighty-six and had battled the effects of pancreatic cancer for eleven years. His body no longer digested and eliminated food normally. He lost the strength to walk to the bathroom. Mentally, he was still sharp, so he predicted a short future.

Gary invited us to his "going away party" three months before his death. We sang his favorite hymn, "Beautiful Savior," and said the Lord's Prayer, and his pastor gave a sermon in Gary's honor. In effect, he wrote his own funeral service, invited relatives and friends, and was pleased with the results. He reminisced about all the beach parties he and Patty had enjoyed at their home on the lake, and he wanted one last barbecue. When he put his home up for sale, I asked him where he would go if the house sold quickly. He answered, "To heaven." His timing was right.

When specialists at Stanford University's medical research center discovered that he was still alive eleven years after Whipple surgery for pancreatic cancer, they asked Gary for his family health history. They also asked if, after death, he would donate his body for research to help others recover from pancreatic cancer. His body was taken to the research center immediately upon death. I'm looking forward to hearing the results. What they won't discover is Gary's determination to stay alive for Patty in her battle with Parkinson's disease and his trust that God would help him in his efforts.

CHAPTER 20

Children Listen and Then They Make Their Own Choices

I raised my boys much the same as I was raised, with a strong work ethic. When Andy was nine, I noticed him watching Saturday morning TV cartoons. He wasn't making the most of his God-given talents. I mentioned that our local newspaper needed people to make deliveries on Saturday mornings and Wednesday evenings. Andy took the initiative to call the newspaper office. Sure enough, he was hired as a newspaper delivery boy for a huge apartment complex. He was thrilled with a regular income plus tips.

When Andy was eleven, his two-year-old brother tried to run along with him to the doors of the apartments. That was a positive experience for Alex, and when he was nine he also applied for a newspaper route.

By this time, Andy, at thirteen, was a bicycle enthusiast. He spent a great deal of time at a bicycle shop on Main Street in Springfield learning how to repair bikes. One day, I got a call from the store manager. He liked Andy very much but knew he was too young for employment, so he asked me if it was okay to hire him to wait on customers and to repair bicycles.

A career began for Andy. He worked at the bike shop during his high school years, especially summers. When he went off to college, he came home to the summer bicycle shop job. One summer, however, he stayed at his fraternity house because he was the academic adviser to his fraternity brothers. He was an all-A student and could help them academically. That summer he was the captain of a river paddleboat on Silver Lake. Now his boating skills paid off.

Andy graduated from Ohio State University with a teaching degree. Doing his student teaching, he became very disenchanted with the discipline problems in the public school system, so he didn't want to pursue a teaching career. He returned to the bike shop, but by this time the company had eight locations and was building another half-million-dollar store. The manager was delighted to offer Andy the management position in the new store.

Andy was there nine years until his wife's career took him to Birmingham, Alabama. Carla earned an undergraduate degree in business management while working at Bank of America. There she trained employees in banking software. She had a similar job waiting for her in Birmingham. The opportunity was too lucrative for Andy to stay at the shop.

Then Andy had the best job of all, taking care of their two little babies, born exactly one year apart. I believed he was too casual with discipline. The children were very curious and touched everything in stores, motels, and restaurants with no restraints. But satisfying their curiosity must have paid off because now that they are in middle school they have achieved beyond their years. Jason and Jackie attended the De Vinci Academy for outstanding students. Now Jason attends North Town STEM (Science, Technology, Engineering, and Mathematics) Middle School and has already taken classes to pass the first year of high school. Both children take part in a competition called Odyssey of the Mind, which is similar to the adult TV show *Jeopardy*. They have gone as far as the international finals.

Andy is a part-time bicycle shop manager on days when the children are in school. Like most parents, he and Carla are on the go. Feeling strained, Andy had a battery of medical tests to determine the cause. Doctors found his thyroid tested positive for an aggressive cancer and another slower-growing cancer. The cancers were caught very early, so there was no problem removing them.

Alex followed in his brother's footsteps. At twelve, he worked with Andy in the bike shop, learning how to repair bikes and to wait on customers. With his background, he was hired by Toys "R" Us to assemble bikes, especially over the Christmas holiday season. During high school he joined a good friend who worked in the kitchen of a local golf and country club. That job prepared him for his new life in Florida. When he learned his dad and I were moving there, he decided he wanted to leave in his third year of college to be with us.

Alex found a job at Mex Southwest, a chain restaurant. The owner realized his management potential and urged him to stay at the restaurant, offering him stock in the company. Most of the employees were students at Florida State University and often failed to show up for work if their class schedules got in the way. As manager, Alex had to fill in for the no-shows and often worked seven days a week. We were discouraged that he dropped out of college, but he was encouraged to make this restaurant his career. We agreed to put up the money for Alex to be a partner with the owner. After seven years, the strain of being on call every day wore on Alex.

When hurricanes destroyed the southwest coast of Florida, Alex accompanied a friend who owned a small handyman business and a truck equipped with tools for home repairs and helped people clean up in neighborhoods damaged by wind and rain. The two didn't ask for money. Those people who could pay paid them very well, and those who couldn't just gave them their thanks. That's how the business was created. Over the next few years their business prospered as they installed storm shutters for people fearing another hurricane.

CHAPTER 21

A Bridge over Troubled Waters

By this time, you may be wondering why it took me so long to convince Jesus to get in my little red sports car and drive away with me to the divorce lawyer's office. I couldn't forget Camelot and all I was taught about doing what Jesus would do. The normal route for someone who wants a divorce would be to divorce, to find someone new, and to remarry, in that order. But you have to understand the mind-set of an abused and controlled individual.

BSS told me early on in the marriage that I was incapable of earning enough money to survive. That was true only because he wouldn't buy me a car so I could leave the house. He controlled the bank accounts, so I was led to believe we had no money. When I eventually had a substantial income, BSS reacted with physical abuse. He had lost control of me. Next, he led me to believe I would go to hell if I filed for divorce.

Three Lutheran ministers told me God was on my side. It was BSS who broke his marital vows to love and to care for me. Other forms of control were threatening to drive my car into a ditch, taking away my health insurance, leaving me with no money, and taking the house away. So I stayed.

Contemplating a divorce, I worried about Andy and Alex. I later learned that they wanted me to divorce sooner. Alex did not respect his father. Perhaps Alex would have drunk less without his dad's influence. Andy has since disowned his dad. He took his two children to BSS's house for an 11:00 a.m. picnic and found him passed out on the front porch with three dogs running loose. He would never let his children be exposed to that again. Andy would invite BSS for Father's Day or for his birthday, but BSS would never show up. Concerned, Andy would drive sixty miles one way to make sure he was okay, only to find him drunk. There have been no more invitations.

Another reason I stayed was because I was raised with the love and care of a large family in Camelot where divorce was not accepted. I did not have an assertive personality. I was and still am very submissive. The last and most important reason I stayed was because I did not feel anyone could love me. I wasn't treated with love by my first husband. Why would I be loved by a second husband? No one would want me. Who would want a brainless jerk like me?

I had casual friends and no serious relationships. I especially liked the group of singles I called the Rat Pack, who gathered at the Regatta Pointe Café at 5:00 p.m. for cocktails. Great for me! I could ride my bike there and back. I didn't even have to carry a purse. I just put a few dollars in my pocket. One time, I had only a fifty-dollar bill to stick in my pocket. It was my girlfriend's birthday and I wanted to buy her a drink. After we all sang happy birthday, I ordered her drink and reached for the money. The fifty-dollar bill must have worked its way out of my pocket while I was pedaling. I biked back to retrace my path but had no luck finding the money. I'm sure I made someone's day!

The Rat Pack consisted of the same fifteen people, give or take a few. One evening, I noticed a new face drinking Amber Bock beer. The next few times the Rat Pack met, Amber Bock wasn't there, but he mysteriously reappeared several months later. He would tell the Pack that he traveled around the country teaching large companies how to increase sales by cutting waste. He could easily have done this from home. Living in Florida for six months with no income tax saved him a lot of money.

This man apparently took an interest in me since I noticed him looking at me from afar no matter where I went in the community. Entering the fitness center, I would see him fishing across the street. When I Rollerbladed, I would spot him biking right around the corner. When we talked at happy hour, he told me he lived in my subdivision. Before long, he was calling me at 7:00 a.m. for breakfast at Bob Evans. Then we were off to the Olympic-size pool for exercise. We would finish by Rollerblading anywhere the paths were smooth. I was okay with Rollerblading but I couldn't swim. He taught me some strokes, which I practiced in five laps while he swam fifty laps in the same amount of time.

Then one day, he didn't leave. He stayed for months. I wasn't used to a man being nice to me. Wherever we went he wanted me on his arm. He thought I was beautiful. In public, I was often mistaken for Farrah Fawcett. He told me I was a special person, but he never told me he loved me. I didn't expect that because I never believed anyone could love me.

Then he disappeared again. I asked the Rat Pack where he was. They said he was with his wife in California. What wife? The next time I saw him I questioned him about his marriage. He told me not to worry, because he was getting a divorce. If you believe that, I have a bridge to sell you.

I called him a bridge because he regarded me as a special person and raised me over troubled waters, but I still was not loved and I hadn't gotten to the other side of the bridge yet. That didn't happen until my second slice of heaven became real.

CHAPTER 22

I'll Never Look Back

I can't help but think that mixing alcohol with mental depression caused BSS's unpredictable behavior. Of course, I would never know because he said I was the problem. We took one more shot at marriage counseling. We each had our own counselor within the same association. I told my counselor the stories I have told you, but I never learned what BSS discussed with his counselor. I didn't care because I had nothing to hide or to be ashamed of.

At our last meeting, my counselor made a startling pronouncement. "I have been in the marriage counseling profession for twenty years," she said, "and I have been committed to helping people keep marriages together. This is the first time I have ever recommended that someone get out and get out fast. This is the worst marriage I've ever counseled. I would like to meet with your husband, not you."

My next step was to speak with a Lutheran minister. I looked on the Internet for a minister with a good reputation in the community. A large parish and school could mean he was well respected and knowledgeable. As a Lutheran schoolteacher, I liked the idea of the large elementary school connected to the church. I was attending a Lutheran church in my neighborhood, but I did not go to my minister for counseling since my story was difficult to tell anyone to whom I was close. The only people who knew my story were Ernest and two friends from Ohio, Polly and Sally, who have stayed connected with me to this day. They encouraged me to write this book, but I found it difficult to put my feelings on paper. Now, as I write, I feel the need to help people like me.

I made an appointment with a minister in Bradenton, Florida. I opened the conversation by noting my lifelong Lutheran background and my twenty-eight years as a schoolteacher. Now my faith was being compromised by a husband who threatened my beliefs. He told me that I would go to hell if I filed for divorce. He also told me that if I divorced him, I would be disobeying my marriage vow to be a faithful wife. I explained to the minister that I wanted a divorce because of the abuse I had suffered for more than forty years. I described many situations to affirm my testimony.

The minister's response was biblically supportive. First, he said, it was my husband who broke his marital vows to love and cherish me. Second, God is loving and merciful. He would not want me to live my life in fear.

With these affirmations from a minister and a marriage counselor, my next step was to find a lawyer who had dealt with spousal abuse. I found a well-established lawyer in Tampa, Florida, who had experience with long-term marriages and who could help me after years of denigration and threats. I had several questions for him. Could BSS really take my home from me? What if he really did drive my car into a ditch? Could he leave me penniless and without health insurance? I took my concerns to God in prayer, saying, "Dear Lord, I trust in your abiding love. You can never and will never leave me or forsake me. Take my hand and lead me."

I arrived at the lawyer's office at 5:00 p.m. a few weeks after I called for an appointment. *He thinks he's busy now,* I thought. *Wait till he meets BSS and me!* My arm was in a soft cast. I hoped he didn't think BSS broke my arm, so I explained that I was recovering from my fourth hand surgery. I wasn't as merciful about BSS's behavior. I described forty years of mental abuse and told how BSS had blamed me for everything from a leaky faucet to his alcoholism.

The next step was disclosure, which included information about careers, debts and credits, investments, savings, and health insurance. Unfortunately, I was never involved in the home budget, so I had little information about that.

During that time, BSS was back living in the house. I didn't think I had the right to change the door locks since his name was on the house title and he was still my husband. Later, I learned that a restraining order could have stopped him from entering. BSS got up in the night to look through my paperwork for information about my lawyer and found that his first name was Dewey. He asked me if Dewey's partners were Hughie and Louie. I have a sense of humor, so I had to laugh before going back to sleep. He also hired a lawyer, a young woman. If I had him pegged right, he thought he could control her too!

One fateful night, BSS spoke the words that finally brought him down: "You are as insignificant as a mosquito. If you do something I don't like, I'll swat you away." Around 4:30 a.m., he whispered in my ear in bed, "I'm going to kill you." I was lying on my side with my eyes wide open, but I didn't move. I didn't know if he had a knife in his hand. I thought if I moved the knife might enter me. I lay motionless until he was gone.

I got up terrified and called my lawyer right away. He didn't reach his office until 4:00 p.m., and we met then. I told him about the night before, and he said, "Listen carefully and do not delay. Tomorrow morning at 8:30 a.m. go to the Manatee County Judicial Court building to room 259 and tell this story. It is very crucial that you go immediately."

Sure enough, the next morning I was at door 259. To my shock, the sign on the door read, "Domestic Violence." *I must be at the wrong door*, I thought. *I'm an educated professional woman. There is no violence in my life. Wake up! You should have known something wasn't right ever since he said, "If you don't marry me I'll drink myself to death."* Now that I understood that putting the blame on me was mental abuse, I accepted the truth. It could happen to anyone. Maybe after reading about what I endured, you will recognize the signs that scream out, "This cannot be tolerated."

I opened the door. In front of me was a desk behind an open window framed with glass paneling. A fifty-year-old woman clerk asked me why I was there. I said, "My lawyer sent me here to tell my story, which began forty years ago."

"Don't tell me about forty years ago," she said. "That doesn't count. You've already forgiven those years. Now write three things your husband said or did in the past two weeks that upset you."

That was easy. She asked me to swear on the Bible that what I wrote was true. I love God. I would not lie to Him. She looked over my statement and told me a judge would be in court at 2:00 p.m. to read the document. She would call at 4:00 p.m. to give me the verdict. Her call came at four on the dot. I'll never forget her words! She said, "This is the first day of the rest of your life. The Manatee County police will come to your house at 8:30 p.m. tonight to deliver a restraining order to your husband and will usher him out of the house within ten minutes."

Sure enough, at 8:30 p.m. a policeman arrived on my driveway while I was waiting in the garage. He knocked on the door. My drunk husband opened the door and slammed it in the officer's face. The officer turned to me and told me to wait at the entrance guardhouse until he told me it was safe to come home. "This is not going to be easy," he said. "I'll give him ten minutes to take what belongings he needs and get out of the house."

I got in the bucket seat of my little red sports car and asked Jesus to join me. He was beginning to like His little bucket seat. The officer came to the guardhouse and gave me the all-clear sign. With a legal restraining order, I changed the locks on the doors so BSS could not come back. He would not return until he broke in after Hurricane Charley.

I later discovered that BSS had taken some of his belongings but had been more interested in taking mine. He had always threatened to leave me penniless, and he was following through on that threat. I had only one credit card in my wallet, and he took it as well as evidence of bank accounts. Without a credit card, I was penniless. I hoped my little red sports car had enough gas to get me to the lawyer's office the next day. Jesus and I went anyway.

My lawyer showed extreme concern about my husband's behavior and took BSS to court pronto. The judge ordered that my credit card be returned to me. BSS disobeyed the order, saying he didn't have the card. The judge held him in contempt of court with a likely jail sentence. I didn't leave the courthouse without my credit card.

BSS tried to get me back by ordering me to court to sell the house. My lawyer was knowledgeable enough to know that BSS could not legally take the house from me. BSS next threatened to take away my health insurance, which he could do because it was in his name. I spent months investigating twenty-two individual health care plans but was rejected because of my four finger arthritis surgeries. That scared me because I needed one more hand surgery, which I hoped would be my last.

Knowing I had insurance until the day of the divorce, I scheduled surgery for August 13, 2004, at Tampa General Hospital fifty miles north of my home. That day the weather forecast for Tampa was devastating. Hurricane Charley was expected to hit the city at 150 mph. The hospital was scheduled to close just when I was anesthetized for surgery, but the storm track suddenly changed as the hurricane approached the state. It struck the northern tip of Captiva Island on Charlotte Harbor and followed the Peace River to Port Charlotte, heading north.

My best friend, Polly, met me at the hospital where her husband dropped her off. She planned to drive my car home and stay with me for ten days until I recovered. I wasn't fully awake when Polly moved me from the hospital into the car. I barely heard her say she couldn't take me home. It was impossible to get through the streets further south. She took me to her home in the Villages, in the middle of Florida. I didn't understand what she was talking about.

I slept for the next three days. Finger surgery is very painful, and the pills were keeping me sleepy. When I woke up, I saw the hurricane destruction on a television news report. Despite having my arm and my hand in a soft cast and a sling, I was anxious to see if my house was damaged. I called Alex, who said he had assessed the damage. Many screens were torn out, and twenty-two tiles were ripped from the roof. Thank God, no windows were broken, but a bedroom window had a hole in the middle as if a stick went through it.

I thanked Polly for her hospitality but asked her to take me home. Driving through the neighborhood, we saw debris from damaged homes piled high along the roads. I cried when I saw my community with the vegetation ripped out. My house was a smelly mess from the defrosted food in the freezer. I had it filled up for Polly and me during my recovery. All the meat had thawed and the juice had run onto the kitchen floor. The bedroom window was completely shattered. There was plastic tape over it with a note reading, "I covered the window for you. Lucas." I guess he fixed it after he broke in.

Just like looters, BSS took the opportunity to check out what was in the house. I'm sure he wanted to see the Corian kitchen countertop, which I replaced after he moved out. He had accused me of buying expensive granite, and he had to pay half of the price because he had burned the countertop cooking. He could see that I had replaced it with the same Corian.

I'm sure BSS also wanted to find evidence of a boyfriend living there. He would have liked to provide that information to his lawyer. I hated to disappoint him. If he was so anxious to help me, why didn't he clean up the meat juice all over the kitchen floor and throw away all the spoiled food since I had only one good arm to use for clean-up?

I figured out why it took so long to get a divorce. Since my attorney charged for every phone call and every visit, the longer it took the more money he made. After two years, we made it to arbitration, but my husband's lawyer never showed up. I wondered how much she charged him for her services. My lawyer, Dewey, was there with bells on. He said he was in a good mood. I still owed him $6,000 and he wiped my slate clean. After listening to BSS complain about how I spent money on food and gas at Walmart, he must have felt sorry for me.

The final decree was bittersweet. My lawyer said I needed to maintain my lifestyle after a forty-year marriage. BSS was ordered to give me half of his pension. I kept my pension. That was quite unusual in Florida, a fifty-fifty state. Everything else that I knew of was split.

I was prepared for BSS to show no mercy with health care. He took my name off of his policy that day. He could have allowed me to stay on COBRA for eighteen months since I couldn't find an individual insurance policy. That may have been another tactic to make me stay in the marriage. He thought I'd change my mind about the divorce if I were denied health insurance. Maybe that's why he asked me to reverse the divorce.

I needed a group policy from a large corporation. A Lowe's Home Improvement Center was being built ten miles down the street from my home. Immediately following the divorce, I walked into a trailer outside the new building where the store was hiring employees. I was hired as a specialist in interior design. Thank You, dear God, for training me to be a creative decorator when I had my basement workstations. Now I know that years ago God was equipping me to live a better life.

CHAPTER 23

What If Tomorrow Never Comes?

Working nine to five at Lowe's Home Improvement Center and clocking in and out were new to me. As a teacher, I was on a yearly salary and pretty much made my own schedule, especially at the college level. As a Lowe's specialist, I had a desk and made appointments for high-dollar interior decorating sales.

On Saturday morning, February 18, 2006, as I walked down an aisle to my desk, I almost fainted, and quickly sat down. I couldn't understand what was wrong with me. It was only seven and my phone was already ringing. It was a Lowe's assistant manager telling me the police were looking for me. He asked me if I was in trouble. "Absolutely not," I said. I had recently sold the Manatee County Police Department forty blinds for its newly painted office building. I was sure someone was calling about the installation date. The assistant manager asked me to come down to the break room.

When I arrived, my cell phone rang. It was Alex's girlfriend. The police had instructed her not to call me, but she did anyway. She told me Alex was dead. I fell to my knees and asked her how that could be. She didn't know. I told her he was at my house the night before installing a new garbage disposal. He left around eight-thirty, holding Valentine cookies in one hand and hugging me with the other, telling me he loved me as he always did.

I got in my car and headed to the boat to tell his father. I wondered how I could cope. In an instant, my life had changed. Nothing could change what happened. Most important, I dwelled on the deep love Alex and I had for each other and especially on the previous night. What else could I do but accept a new life? Losing a child brought the most devastating pain I had ever experienced, but in time God gave me the peace that passes all understanding.

When I told his father, we agreed to go together to Alex's apartment to find out what happened. The apartment was roped off with yellow tape like a crime scene. Questioning Alex's girlfriend, we found out that they had partied the night before in a bar with friends. Alex had drunk several beers and rum. His buddy had six methadone prescription pills, and one was missing. No one knew how or if it got in Alex's drink, but the drug killed him.

My best source of information was the coroner. He said the results would not be known for three months, but he confided in me. He was so sorry for me and realized I needed to know the truth. There was a high level of alcohol in Alex's body but a small amount of the drug. There were no other drugs in his body. I asked the coroner how it was possible for such a small amount of the drug to kill Alex. He explained that novices can tolerate less of a drug than regular users can.

Out of frustration, I called the boy responsible for handling the prescription drug. There was no answer, so I left a message. I never expected him to return my call. In tears, he called me back. He was so shaken up I didn't have to ask him how this happened; his reaction let me know. I told him never to let something like that happen again.

Needing to know more details about that fateful night, I spoke further with Alex's girlfriend. Apparently, Alex's dog, Max, knew more than anybody. When Alex threw up black blood in the bathroom and fell against the door, Max tried desperately to get into the bathroom to help his master.

Hearing that, I reminisced about the time Alex brought Max for a ride on the sailboat. Alex found Max at the Humane Society after he had been rescued from an abusive owner. His left foreleg was crippled and bandaged to protect open sores. When Alex went to the bow to release the lines, he told Max to stay in the cockpit. He sat very still and watched every move Alex made, ready to rescue him at a moment's notice. When Alex returned to the cockpit, Max hugged and kissed him as dogs do so well. His tail wagged for everybody.

Some humans should take lessons from our four-legged friends on how to care for others. When Alex died, Max was beside himself. I wished his girlfriend had been as concerned. When he realized Alex's fate, Max ran away from home, never to return. I followed Max's example and left home to stay with Gary and Patty. I couldn't stay away forever like Max, but I came home with peace in my heart.

What would I have done without Ernest at my side after Alex's death? I called him in distress, and he came right over only to find me lying on the kitchen floor. I told him I wanted to be with Alex. I will never forget his words. "You will," he said, "but not tonight." Then when would I be with him? How could I survive the days without him? I had to tell myself to concentrate on the here and now, not the hereafter.

I couldn't stop the nightmares. In each dream, I was trying to save my son. In one, I was walking down a sidewalk when I came upon a clear piece of concrete. I could see Alex trapped under it, but I couldn't save him. In recent years, my dreams of Alex have turned to joy and laughter, especially when I remember him as a toddler. One of my fondest memories is the way he communicated before he could talk. If he saw something he wanted to tell me about, he would hold my head and turn it in the direction he wanted me to look.

When I saw Alex in the casket he looked so fit and healthy. I fell to the floor. Whose feet did I see? Ernest's! He gently picked me up as if he were God's angel. At this point, I didn't know what to say to God. Even He couldn't change what happened. I asked Him to help me accept my loss.

Gary and Patty, Ernest, Alex's father, my son's girlfriend, and I set sail on *Steadfast* to spread Alex's ashes over Tampa Bay at the spot where he had caught a monster tarpon. His ashes were in a biodegradable shell about two feet in diameter. We put the shell in the water but it did not sink. We threw beautiful flowers in the water as we circled around the shell. The boat's wake created quite a stir, and the shell tipped on its side. Just then a dolphin jumped over the shell and they both went down together. God sent His angel to take Alex home.

*   *   *

I was so distraught at work that I asked the store manager whether he would hire me back if I left for three months. He said, "Absolutely." I went to stay at the cottage down on the shoreline from Gary and Patty on Lake Tahoe. That was where I found peace in my soul. The Serenity Prayer by theologian Reinhold Niebuhr was and still is my hope. It goes like this: "God grant me the serenity to accept the things I cannot change, courage to change the things I can, and wisdom to know the difference." I couldn't change Alex's death, so I accepted it. I could change the marriage I had, and I did. God had given me the wisdom to go on.

Having just lost Jeff, Gary and Patty were quite understanding. We talked about the sons we lost. In time, I learned to accept

God's plan for Alex. He was born under a black thundercloud and couldn't help but feel the drizzle. He battled the depression that also plagued his grandmother and his father. Adding alcohol was a recipe for disaster. I could see this coming. In His mercy, I believe God saved me from a life of grief. My other son, Andy, found a silver lining in the clouds. He emulated all my brothers and chose their attitude toward life. Unlike his father, he drank only in moderation.

That summer I stayed with Gary. He seemed awfully tired. We agreed that at seventy-six it was okay for him to take a nap in the afternoon while I went biking around Lake Tahoe and Rollerblading on the sidewalks of Sand Harbor. By February, the whites of his eyes were turning yellow and his urine was brown. His primary physician suspected pancreatic cancer.

The local hospitals didn't have the expertise to perform the necessary surgery. Gary's daughter, a former Stanford University Hospital oncology nurse, recommended a pancreatic cancer surgeon at Stanford. Gary got a second opinion and was scheduled for surgery sooner rather than later. I prayerfully waited for the results. The surgeon not only removed the cancer but half each of Gary's stomach, liver, pancreas, intestines, and the lymph nodes in the surrounding area.

Between Gary's surgery and his six-week checkup, Ernest was fatally injured in a car accident.

What would I have done differently if I had known I would never see Ernest again? I would have said those three words, "I love you," that are so difficult to express. I would have offered more thank-yous for all the times he rescued me from life's torments. But I have no regrets because my need for him to be close at hand told Ernest how much I loved him, and I knew he loved me because he was always there for me, no matter when or where.

Ernest did not have an easy life after meeting Nanette.

He dated her nine years before deciding to marry her. She was intelligent, a class valedictorian, but often did not use common sense. She had outbursts of anger and uncontrollable laughter. When their son, Mikey, was born, she went into a deep depression.

Mom opened her revolving door once again to care for Mikey, but that was not an easy task at her age. She had a hernia that erupted when she tried to carry the baby. I offered to help Ernest by caring for Mikey until Nanette recovered, which she did quite quickly. The reason for her unpredictable behavior went undiagnosed for several years. We didn't know that her mental problems were physical until one Easter morning.

I have learned to live as if tomorrow will never come for me or for others. I do not mean to dwell on the negative but to encourage the positive. I want to care for and love people while I still can. I live my life as if I will never have another chance to shake someone's hand and say, "God bless you." For myself, I try to achieve today what I may not be able to do tomorrow.

PART III

A SECOND SLICE
OF HEAVEN

CHAPTER 24

When My Old Life Ended
and a New Life Began

My life began when I met Clark Lewis Armstrong on March 28, 2005. We took jobs at Lowe's for different reasons. I was divorced and needed health insurance. I needed to work for a large corporation that offered a group policy. Clark hired on at Lowe's to increase his Social Security benefits since he had received none as a government employee.

Clark became a kitchen designer while I was an interior designer. Both positions required extensive training. Like most goody-two-shoes girls, I sat in front of the class; he was in the back with the bad boys. I turned around and noticed him looking at me. Wow! I barely noticed that he was handsome. Getting to know him was easy since he was such a friendly guy.

Since Clark was a retired Ohio State Highway Patrol lieutenant, had handled security for the governor of Ohio, and had been a police chief, I told him about my ex-husband's abusive behavior during our forty-year marriage. I thought he would understand. In conversation, I learned he was unhappily married to a woman who owned a towing company. He joked that in the winter it snowed green in Ohio between US-75 and US-71. She claimed to be the bitch from hell, so we named her the Beloved

Daughter of Satan (BDS). I also found myself asking Clark for help after Ernest's tragic accident.

Ernest loved and cared for me my whole life. He would move right beside me from state to state. He was there for me when BSS got out of control in Ohio, and I was there for him when his wife, Nanette, fell into a coma at thirty-eight.

On an Easter morning, I brought Mom out of the nursing home to be with family at church. I was waiting for Ernest, Nanette, and Mikey to arrive at church when I received a phone call. Nanette had suffered an aneurysm in the personality section of her brain.

We should have guessed years earlier that she had a problem. The veins on one side of her brain were knotted and had burst open. The blood flowed from one side of the brain to the other, affecting her body positioning. The left side of her body was straight and rigid, while the right side was in the fetal position. This would never change. Nanette's temperature was so high that she was put on a block of ice to keep her alive.

During this difficult time, I gave Ernest's thirteen-year-old son a temporary home when he didn't know where to turn. Nanette lived in a nursing home for twenty-eight years with 98 percent of her brain cells dead. To support Ernest, I would often go to the nursing home with him. It was hard to tell if Nanette knew we were there, because her eyes moved so rapidly. She couldn't speak. In my heart, I believed or wanted to believe she knew we were there. She died of ovarian cancer at sixty, unable to tell her caretakers of any pain or symptoms. In God's mercy, I hope she died peacefully.

Ernest bought a condo just two blocks from me in Bradenton. He would drive back and forth from Ohio, bringing a load of furniture each time. Six months after Alex died, Ernest brought his final load, which included Mom's cherry table with a black marble top and a Queen Ann chair for me. His first night back, we celebrated with a lasagna casserole dinner. We ate only half, so we planned another dinner the next night at five-thirty.

The time came and went with no sign of Ernest. It was not like him to pass up a homemade meal. By eight that night, I was looking for him. When I got home, there was a message on my phone. It was Mikey, who said, "My dad was killed on State Road 64 at 10:30 this morning."

I thought in my heart, *Please God, not Ernest. What would I do without my guardian angel? God, had Ernest fulfilled his purpose in life? He took such good care of his wife before she died. He helped me get back on my feet again. Was it part of Your plan to take him home to heaven?* I was left behind, wishing Ernest had lived to see my second slice of heaven.

Coming to my senses, I called Mikey back. He explained what happened to his father. Ernest never liked to be at home on Monday mornings when the noisy lawn service workers mowed the grass, so he drove north on State Road 64 to get a newspaper and breakfast. An eighteen-year-old boy was heading south on the road. He bent down to look for his map because he had missed the Bradenton exit. He swerved over the double yellow lines and hit Ernest's car head-on. Neither driver had time to brake.

Ernest flew out of his open window, and his car rolled over him in a ditch. His head landed with so much force that the letter *w* from the word *water* on a drain was embedded in his forehead. The boy was helicoptered to Tampa General Hospital where he was treated for minor injuries. His driver's license was suspended for one year—a small price to pay for a life.

I had to make many quick decisions. What about the car? Where were Ernest's personal belongings? What about a funeral? Where would he be buried? His Ford SUV was towed away. The state police advised me not to look at the car, so I asked my friend

Clark from Lowe's if he would search for Ernest's belongings in the wreckage. He did but found nothing.

Soon after, I received a call from the state trooper office to come and get Ernest's wallet, which I saved for Mikey. When I arrived, I asked troopers if Ernest was wearing his seat belt. They showed me the pictures of his seat belt in the recoiled position—in other words, not used. That was surprising to me since I always saw him wear his seat belt. Ernest's body was cremated in Florida and buried in the family plot in Lake Tahoe.

Gary helped with the funeral plans although he was scheduled to be at Stanford Hospital for his six-week checkup that week. He asked me if I could get the ashes to Lake Tahoe by the weekend. The cemetery overlooked the lake and was just down the street from Gary's home. I called the mortician, who said we were cutting it close, but he would try. The timing was so close that the very hot urn was transferred from one car to another on I-75.

Two days later, I was at the hospital to be with Gary and Patty for his checkup. Gary could see the sorrow in my eyes. He gave me words of strength and encouragement about his prognosis. He told me not to cry for him. He had lived a very happy life and he was not afraid to die. I looked at Patty, who was looking longingly at Gary. Her left hand was shaking uncontrollably. Words could not express my sadness as I had Ernest's ashes in one arm and held Gary in my other arm, thinking he could have only three months to live. And why was Patty trembling so badly?

Gary planned a beautiful memorial service at the cemetery. We placed the urn next to Jeff's grave. I tossed Ernest's well-worn baseball cap over the urn and buried it with him. He wore it so long that the blue faded to tan.

If ever I could find humor in a funeral service it was in the eulogies by two women who professed to love Ernest, though not in a romantic way. He was everybody's friend. I wondered what his two girlfriends in Florida would think about that. Three months after his funeral I received a letter from a gal living in Montana who wrote about her love for Ernest. I could understand that. He helped anyone and everyone in every way.

To this day, Ernest's neighbors still talk about what a great guy he was. Even BSS found a friend in him. Ernest brought out the best in Lucas. That was one funeral BSS felt was worth his efforts to attend.

CHAPTER 25

Welcome to Paradise

It was time to return to Florida. But why? Everyone I had brought with me was gone. Losing Alex and Ernest would have been almost unbearable if it not for God's abiding grace. The divorce was meant to be and brought me peace. Still, I felt alone, so I began talking to God more often.

He must have been at work when Andy called and pleaded with me to come to Birmingham, Alabama, to be with him and his family. He had found a fifties-plus community in my price range close to his home. The problem was that my present home had fallen in value by $50,000 due to the recession. I would have to wait for house values to rise, and that didn't happen very fast.

I had other reasons to stay in Florida. I needed to work at Lowe's for the health insurance. My gynecologist insisted that I have my ovaries removed since my sister had died from ovarian cancer and cancer was running rampant in my family.

Another reason to stay in Florida was that my relationship with Clark was growing. When I was on sick leave from Lowe's to have my ovaries removed, he stopped by the house to bring me a card and a bouquet of flowers. The card was signed by many of my coworker buddies. I told Clark to tell everyone thanks for the beautiful flowers and the card. He confessed that the flowers were from him. That was the first message I got from him that he cared for me.

Then one day Clark didn't show up at Lowe's for work. Rumor had it that he suffered a heart attack while on vacation in Ohio. Days and weeks passed. I didn't know if he was dead or alive. I felt an emptiness inside. I had experienced the deaths of many people and thought I could be strong, but this time was different. Six weeks went by and there he was at Lowe's automated door coming to work. My heart leaped for joy the minute I saw him.

Clark's heart surgeon suggested he stop smoking, so he looked a few pounds heavier but just as handsome as ever. He explained that for three days he had symptoms such as the need to burp and finally entered a hospital in Cincinnati, Ohio. A heart surgeon and his staff were immediately put on call. Clark was having a heart attack as they prepared to insert two stents in the arteries going in and out of his heart. I wondered why I felt so much emotion on hearing this when we had just a casual relationship.

Clark would occasionally stop by on his golf cart for a chat. Once he fixed my kitchen sink faucet. Another time he found me in the backyard trying to trim palmetto palm branches. He told me I needed better branch cutters, so he went home and brought me back his tool. I went to town on those branches, bundled them, and carried them to the street. My arms were itchy from the sap. I took a shower, but overnight the sap spores spread to my legs and torso. The next day at work my buddies thought I had shingles. Clark said I better see a doctor. The itchy rash was spreading rapidly.

In the exam room the nurse asked me what she could do for me. I lifted my T-shirt and she ran from the room, screaming for the doctor. Within five minutes of seeing me, the doctor got me an appointment with an allergist, who wrote me three prescriptions and recommended bed rest. I was having trouble breathing and was suffering chest pains.

A few days later, I was well enough to thank Clark for his bush clippers, but he didn't speed over to pick them up. For some reason, he didn't want to get too close to me. He did want to tell me he was thinking about divorcing BDS. I said, "If you do that I will never betray you." So began our love affair.

At this point in my life, I knew the kind of man I didn't want. Clark had all the characteristics I did want. We agreed on everything—the clothes we wore, the food we ate, the style of car we wanted, the decisions we made on financial matters, but most important, how we wanted to spend the rest of our lives together. I had heard it said that opposites attract. I had just ended a marriage that proved the adage wrong. Clark and I enjoyed our similarities and our good times working together.

I always spent my summers at the cottage on Lake Tahoe, and now I asked Clark to come with me. I had extended the invitation, but I knew he couldn't accept. His relationship with his wife had long since died, but he was still married. Then came the words that changed my life forever: "I'm flying to Lake Tahoe to see you."

Clark was caught leaving his house with suitcase in hand. He would never make a return trip. He boarded a flight from Tampa, Florida, to Atlanta, where he changed to a Delta flight to Chicago, and then on to Reno-Tahoe Airport, Nevada. The flight took thirteen hours. I picked him up at midnight. When Clark walked down the concourse, my heart burst with the love I had for him. He made a giant leap for me. How could I ever thank him enough?

The trip from Reno-Tahoe Airport to the cottage was not what Clark had expected. He offered to drive but only I knew the dirt road by heart. A two-lane road took us by the Schmidt (my maiden name) Preserve, the five-hundred-plus acres Gary donated to Douglas County. The land was bordered by a river for canoeing. Originally, there was a hunting lodge for overnight guests, and now there were hiking paths for Boy Scouts and Girl Scouts. To preserve the natural beauty of the land, Gary specified that no building take place.

From there we turned onto Lakeshore Drive, the road that circled Lake Tahoe. The lake has been named the most beautiful lake in the United States, the second being Lake Charlevoix in Michigan. Clark was getting curious about where the trip would end. We turned onto a mile-long dirt road, barely one lane, bordered by pines, birch trees, and deer staring at our headlights.

A cottage with a cobblestone fireplace appeared on a hill in the woods overlooking a sandy beach. On the grounds were several large stones to build a fire pit, and there was plenty of dead wood. The lake, more than five hundred feet deep, was aqua blue. The cobblestone fireplace took up the whole west wall of the cottage, and the other walls were covered with cedar wood or kitchen cabinets. The place was rustic but very alluring.

After traveling thirteen hours by plane, Clark was so tired he could hardly walk. We decided to begin our sightseeing the next day and to get some rest that night. The bedroom was tiny and had only one double bed. We had never slept together before, so I had no idea Clark snored so loudly. It must have been the change in atmosphere. I would never hear him snore like that again.

The events of the day were tiring for sixty-year-olds. To add insult to injury, Clark had to get up in the night to use the bathroom. Do you know how dark it is in the forest? The only light came from the stars and the moon. He had to feel the walls to find the bathroom, wherever that was. He was beginning to believe it was outside. I felt sorry for him but laughed at him at the same time.

As the days went by, we left the real world behind. We water-skied, fished from a rowboat, and swam in the lake, never thinking that soon we would have to face the music back in Florida, with an imminent divorce for Clark and a stunned community ready to throw us under the bus. Were we equipped for all that?

Now we had to face reality. We could never return to the way we were before. Clark moved into my house. He could do nothing else. Was he prepared to live with a woman reeling from an abusive marriage? I was told that because of this marriage, I could never love a man. I questioned whether I could accept Clark's love. I questioned whether he could love me after all I'd been through. Maybe he loved me now, but what about later when he realized my faults? Like BSS, would he start calling me an asshole and a jerk when he discovered I was not perfect? Would he have an affair with another woman as BSS did? I was still the same bumbling idiot I was before, only older and not so pretty.

My fears became reality. I began crying in the night. Clark didn't know how to deal with it. One night, he left to go to the boat. *Oh no. This can't happen again*, I thought, but he came back, saying, "I love you. We will make this work." Those words made me realize I had nothing to fear. I stopped the tears and came to terms with the failures of my first marriage. It was not all my fault. Clark eased my mind by saying he admired all the traits I was criticized for in my first marriage, especially my determination to accomplish my goals. I adopted Clark's laid-back attitude, confident that a job would get done in due time. We learned from each other.

When I realized Clark and I were committed to each other, I wanted him to know everything about my past. Secrets aren't fair. He knew about my unhappy marriage and I knew about his. His wife's money didn't bring him happiness. He wanted to love and to be loved. Above all, he wanted a relationship with God, which his former marriage did not inspire.

On a workday for me and a free day for Clark, I handed him a bag of notes and scribbles that I had made to document my relationship with BSS over forty years. When I got home he gave me a look of disbelief. He questioned what kind of man I had been married to. I believe Clark loved me more for being honest with him. He became the biggest supporter of my plan to use the notes to write this book.

When we met, I also told Clark about the sexual disease I had inherited from BSS forty years earlier. I had had clear Pap smears until I was fifty-eight years old. I had heard that human papilloma could cause cancer in later years. Sure enough, an annual exam showed that the disease from many years ago had caused precancer cells. Every six months I was carefully checked.

I shared this with Clark. He would accompany me into the examination room. He was alarmed when I had to sign papers to approve the removal of cancer if found. He hadn't realized the seriousness of the illness. He faithfully took me for the exams until the risk diminished and finally disappeared. Was I lucky? Some people would call me blessed. I would rather believe that this was one more of God's miracles. I don't take my faith lightly. I had yet to see the greatest miracle of my life.

CHAPTER 26

Love Your Neighbor as Yourself

We settled into our life together. We were an island unto ourselves. Of course, we had to deal with the rumors about our love affair. The worst source of treachery was Clark's wife. She fought us every inch of the way. When Clark would ask for his personal belongings she would say she couldn't find them or had found only half of them.

He asked for his father's grandfather clock; she gave it to him without the key. He asked for his Thomas Kincaid oil paintings; she turned them over without the documentation. He asked for his gun collection; she delivered it without the ammunition. Worst of all, she claimed she could not find his dress diamond ring, worth thousands.

Clark looked for an honest, helpful divorce lawyer, which proved a difficult task. We had hoped for a quick and easy resolution through We the People, a group of pro bono lawyers who settled divorces between consenting parties. How silly of us. That would never happen! Clark called his wife BDS (Beloved Daughter of Satan) because she found a lawyer who lied and cheated his way to court, draining all finances in a long, ugly battle.

Clark settled for less after a year, so the divorce was finalized. She asked for ninety days to find health insurance. Seems to me she should have done that a year earlier. Clark gave her the ninety days and then some. She took him back to court over a life insurance policy with a cash value of $1,500. She thought she would get $26,000. Unfortunately for her, he wasn't dead yet. The judge threw her out of court, saying the divorce had already been granted and he didn't want to see her again.

Loving an ex-spouse is hard, but loving your neighbor as yourself sometimes seemed harder after I met Merry. I have since forgiven Merry for her improprieties. Our relationship started when she moved next door to us in Bradenton, Florida. It was the Halloween season and I found a pumpkin filled with candy on my front porch. Nice gesture, but there was a catch. I had to refill the pumpkin and give it to the next neighbor. I was guilty of breaking the chain because I didn't get the next pumpkin to someone on a timely basis due to my work schedule. I must have disappointed Merry.

Merry loved the holidays. She threw an Easter party for the neighborhood. With spoons carrying fresh eggs dangling from our mouths, we hopscotched down her driveway to see who could reach the end without smashing the eggs. Best of all was the Easter egg hunt. Merry had hidden the eggs in the bushes the night before, but no one could find them in the morning. We knew the snakes enjoyed that Easter breakfast.

Merry was particularly bothered when I had new carpeting installed in my living room and bedroom. A few days later, she saw me fixing the concrete between my front porch and the sidewalk. I had to apply the cement before it hardened, so I didn't stop to talk when she came over. She didn't recognize my time constraints. She wanted to know how I liked the carpet, what the color and the texture were, and where I put it. I told her it was lovely and kept working. She didn't get to see it and was disappointed.

Before Clark's arrival, my status as a single woman was a mystery for Merry. She couldn't stand it when she saw a white Mustang convertible in my driveway. She just had to see who was in my house. She would knock on the door, but Alex and I didn't let her in. We thought she was being snoopy. He also had an old-style Jeep with canvas sides. Now she was sure I was dating a beach bum. Alex got a big laugh out of that.

Things kept getting worse. I couldn't rely on my little red sports car to get to Birmingham, Alabama, to visit Andy and his family. Andy was selling his royal blue Buick sedan because he had bought an SUV, which was better transportation for his two children. I bought the sedan and parked it in my driveway back in Florida. Merry spread the news around the community that a man who drove a blue Buick was staying with me.

Now the plot thickened. Along came my handsome Clark in his black S10 pickup truck. Or was it his Infinity sedan, or could it have been his red golf cart, or maybe his Cadillac SUV? He owned all four. Merry would knock on the door to see all the different men. We decided to lock the door.

Once after the loss of Alex I left the door unlocked. Ernest called me to find out how I was doing. I was in tears over my loss, so he drove his tan SUV Buick over to my house. Ernest found me weeping on the kitchen floor. He bent over me and tried to soothe my broken heart. Just then, Merry walked in. She got what she wanted. She saw a man bending over me. Now she had fuel for her gossip. She was kind enough to bring me a crying shawl but asked for it back two weeks later. Strange!

Merry had no mercy on me. She wouldn't give up. She called me and said she had something to discuss. I asked her what it was. She said she would be waiting on my patio to talk about it. Merry didn't seem to care that I was on my way to a doctor's appointment. This would often happen.

Thinking we could discourage this behavior, Clark and I agreed to meet with Merry and her husband. During our conversation, she pointedly looked at Clark and told him she was so happy that after all the men I'd had in and out of the house I had finally settled on him. I said, "Excuse me?" Merry's husband quickly change the topic. Soon after, she moved back to Michigan, but she would return to haunt me.

CHAPTER 27

Our Vows to Love One Another

It wasn't hard to decide that we wanted to marry in the little Lutheran church in Sand Harbor, Lake Tahoe, where Clark came back to God. We were anxious to return to the cottage after a year. It was just as enchanting as before. We spent a month there finalizing our wedding plans. We decided to create our own unique ceremony. Traditionally, the bride and groom each hold a lighted candle and light one common candle to signify their unity. We changed fire to water.

On our way to the Sand Harbor cottage, we stopped at Lido Beach in Sarasota, Florida, to capture salt water from the Gulf of Mexico. We took our beach chairs to enjoy the afternoon. Clark brought a jar into waist-deep water, dipped down to fill it, and stood up. I was waiting for a dove to sit on his head. If I didn't know better, I'd say he looked like Jesus being baptized by John the Baptist in the River Jordan.

It was a cloudy day, drizzly and dreary, not a good day for sunbathers. We enjoyed the serenity. I put my head back and looked into the sky. This was the moment I saw my first and only vision, Jesus Christ on the cross. The vision was as clear as a black-and-white photograph. It was so vivid that I could see the crown of thorns on His head and the blood drops on His forehead. His eyes were looking heavenward. I asked Clark to look up to the sky. He saw the same thing and was mesmerized. The image was as clear to him as it was to me.

Why would God show us Jesus suffering on a cross? What was the vision's meaning for our lives? I can only guess that He said, "Here is My Son. I sacrificed Him for you because I love you." How could we not love Him back? The vision made us want to dedicate our marriage and our lives to God's purposes. Now we reach out and touch the hand of God as He leads us through peaceful waters or stormy seas.

Leaving Florida, we went north to the Great Lakes, where we both grew up, and scooped a cup of fresh water from Lake Erie. It was interesting to see that the waters looked identical in the jars despite the different locations. We intended to pour a cup of each water into one container to symbolize our unity and our love for the lakes and the oceans.

We had a pre-wedding day dinner at the Harbor View Yacht and Country Club where Gary had a membership. All forty wedding guests were invited. After thirty days of ninety-degree weather, the temperature dropped to fifty-five degrees with a tempest on Lake Tahoe and pounding rain. The dinner went from outdoor baloneys overlooking the yacht basin to indoor candlelight and fireplaces. It couldn't have worked out better. The atmosphere was warm and friendly.

We were married the next day, September 4, 2010. Gary was thrilled to walk me down the aisle and to give me away to Clark. Jokingly, I told him he couldn't wear his rubber thongs but had to put on real shoes. Despite his wealth he was a humble man. The next day, Clark and I spoke our wedding vows to each other.

Clark's Vow

Maggie, with all my heart, I take you to be my wife, to share the good times and hard times as one. With all my heart, here in the presence of God, our family, and friends, I pledge to be forever faithful and honest to you and to love you more with each passing day.

Just as this ring I give you today is a circle without end, representing my deepest true love for you, my commitment to you will never fail. Let these three diamonds represent our faith in God—God the Father, God the Son, and God the Holy Spirit.

Maggie, thee I wed.

Maggie's Vow

Clark, I give you this ring. Wear it with love and joy.

I love you, Clark.

In the presence of God, our family, and friends, I take you to be my partner in life and my one true love. I will cherish our love more today than I did the day before. I will trust and respect you, laugh with you, and cry with you, loving you faithfully through obstacles we may face together.

I give you my hand, my heart, and my love from this day forward as long as we live.

We wrote these words from our hearts. The music, prayers, and Bible passages had special meaning in our lives. The reception was held at Gary's daughter's estate on a hillside overlooking Lake Tahoe. Later, back at the simple little cottage, we enjoyed a campfire with guests on the beach and rowed on the lake. I was finally at peace. In my wildest dreams, I never would have guessed my life would change so much. Thank goodness I never gave up. Thank You, God, for giving me this slice of heaven.

CHAPTER 28

Lending Hands

We slowly weaned ourselves from working at Lowe's, going from full time to part time to no time. It wasn't long before we devised a way to use the creative and industrial skills we learned through life and at Lowe's. We developed our own company, called Lending Hands–Skills to Meet Your Needs.

We started with a bang by painting walls, doors, and trim inside a neighbor's house. She was so pleased with our work that she showed her home to other neighbors, who in turn hired us to paint, wallpaper, upholster, and do minor electric and plumbing repairs. Our specialty was flooring, anything from ceramic and vinyl tile to laminates and painted concrete.

Our next best advertisement was our business cards with a picture of a man's hand holding a hammer. A couple from England picked up that card in a local fitness center and gave us a call. That call was the key to our success. Steve, the owner of one of the largest local homes, asked us to oversee his vacation property in Florida while he was in London.

The list of responsibilities included monitoring pool maintenance, air conditioning, exterior painting, and grounds landscapers. When he and wife learned about our creative skills, they also had us redo most of their furniture with a colonial distressed finish. We upholstered all of the lanai chairs and a settee and painted patio wicker furniture. We've even tailored Steve's business suits, put up their Christmas tree, and decorated their home before their winter vacation.

We also have the responsibility of renting the property when it's not in use by the owner. We have had it rented for the past five years at a 10 percent commission. Clark and I will also oversee the construction of a cottage on the couple's adjacent extra lot.

With that experience on our résumé, we have been hired by a Pennsylvania couple who own five hundred properties around the world, one of which is located in our community. Their home is by far larger and more expensive than all the other homes. Its primary asset is an indoor salts pool surrounded by fifteen-foot palm trees that extend to the upper level. Our recent job was to get a child's car-shaped bed up the circular stairway to a bedroom next to the master bedroom overlooking the downstairs pool.

This client has needs similar to those of our friends from England, so between the two properties we have a lot to handle. We slowly turned over our Lending Hands clients to competing companies and kept just a few long-term customers who depended on us, especially the two estates.

We also used our handyman skills in our own home. We tore out our master bathroom. The most fun was breaking up the old bathtub and shower and ripping off the wallpaper. We wallpapered and installed mirrors and a new toilet while contractor friends put in new cabinets and sinks and tiled in a bathtub and a shower.

We transformed the look of the whole house by tearing out the wall between the kitchen and a bedroom on the back side. We put a snack bar between the two rooms. It was long enough for four bar stools, but we wanted larger, more comfortable chairs with backs, so only three chairs would fit.

Remember how much Jesus liked to ride in my little red sports car? He took one look at that third chair next to Clark and me and made Himself comfortable. He especially enjoys the wide-screen television visible in the adjoining family room. When we watch our Bible study film series He joins us for appetizers and a glass of wine. He's always there when we need Him. He hears our table prayers, and He tells His Father how thankful we are to have Him beside us.

I dread the thought of losing Clark, but as we age we have to face reality. I think of the three chairs at the snack bar. I can picture myself sitting there alone with a broken heart and reaching out for Jesus's hand on one side and Clark's hand on the other to hold me up. C. S. Lewis said the only way to be sure not to have your heart broken is never to give it to anyone. I prefer to believe that it is better to have loved and lost than never to have loved at all.

CHAPTER 29

Our Second Home

If anything could bring our children closer to us, it was the purchase of Ernest's condominium. His son, Mikey, put it up for sale just after Ernest's death. Unfortunately, with the recession in 2008, the market wasn't the best. After the condo had been available for more than a year, Clark and I offered Mikey fair-price value plus a bonus for property on a golf course. He was happy to get rid of the condo, and we were glad to keep it in the family.

We have made it available to family and friends at no cost. Clark's two children and Andy stay there when we don't have a renter in season from January to April. Clark's daughter spends three vacations a year with us in sunny Florida. In fact, she was married on our English friends' beautiful grounds and stayed at the condo. Clark's son is just starting to leave the job behind and enjoys staying at the condo where the fishing is alluring. Andy visits us a few times a year, skirting around the renters.

The condo has two bedrooms, two bathrooms, a living room with a separate dining room, a snack bar separating the kitchen and living room, plus a lanai and a two-car garage. Family members have access to a golf course in the backyard, a pool close by, golf carts, bicycles, a local pub, a restaurant, and parents just around the corner. The kids like the amenities. Most of all, they like the freedom to come and go as they please while enjoying daily pool time and dinners with family. We also appreciate that. At our age, we're late to wake up in the morning and early to bed at night.

The condo pays for itself with renters three months out of the year. Mostly, our renters take care of the place as if it were their own home. Our present renters leave many of their belongings in the garage in anticipation of the next season.

Only one renter has disappointed us. Her name was Merry. Yes! She was the next-door neighbor who moved back to Michigan. She decided she wanted to vacation in Florida and to rent our condo for six months. Wow! A six-month rental was a lot of money. I guess our greed was greater than our common sense. We signed a contract that she and her husband broke in three weeks. Then we were stuck with no renters that season. We should have asked for full payment up front. As it turned out, we were blessed to have these two leave.

When she arrived, I asked Merry if the accommodations were adequate and if she needed anything. She mentioned a number of unconventional items including pans of certain sizes. I pointed out a full set of Farberware pots and pans in the kitchen cabinet. She got angry and said, "How would you know that? You don't live here. I do."

Merry made renovations forbidden in the contract, such as stickers on the walls, some of which tore off the wallboard. She also wanted to install a flag holder on the outdoor garage wall. I asked her not to do that. She said I was not patriotic. Merry called the condo association for approval of the flag holder installation, which she got, but as the owner, I had the last word. I don't know why she didn't just stick the flag in the grass.

Most upsetting was Merry's decision to dispose of items in the condo that she didn't want. At that point, I had a discussion with her husband. We would have to charge them for the missing items. He was sympathetic and said he was trying his best to rescue the items from the trash. It became clear that Merry thought her husband had purchased the home for her and I was interfering. Knowing her past mental problems, I realized her illness had progressed. Her husband bought an RV and canceled the contract. After they left, we noticed severe damage to furniture and found dirt covered with paper towels. They asked for their five-hundred-dollar deposit to be returned. To replace a damaged overstuffed chair and an ottoman alone cost more than five hundred dollars, and what about the $12,000 rent we lost? They were dreaming!

CHAPTER 30

Boats Are Holes in the Water
You Pour Money Into

Make no mistake. God had a plan that Clark and I would someday find ourselves together. It began when Clark was born on February 18, 1947. I was born one year earlier on February 25, 1946. God created parallel paths for us to follow. In our early years, Clark and I ventured out with our dads on the Great Lakes on our boats for fun and fishing. In midlife, each with our own families, we boated to Sandusky Bay most summer weekends. The chances are pretty good that we saw each other!

God gave us similar lifestyles, but it wasn't time for us to be together yet. In our retirement, Clark brought his forty-seven-foot Carver powerboat and I brought a forty-foot sailboat to Tampa Bay, Florida. In my divorce settlement, I kept the house, and BSS was awarded the sailboat where he continued to live.

Clark motored his powerboat down the Tennessee Tombigbee Waterway to the Gulf of Mexico and into Riverview Marina. What a spectacular sight when the boat entered the marina harbor! As a friend so appropriately said, "I've never been on a yacht before." Neither had I. In the main salon were leather sofas, La-Z-Boy chairs, and a dining room table that popped up out of the floor. I was amazed by the upright refrigerator in the kitchen as well as the oven with a cook top, a coffeemaker, and a microwave. There were two staterooms with attached full-size bathrooms. Captain Clark steered the boat from his lounge three decks above the swim platform.

We'd fuel up and find overnight dockage at local ports. That made for pretty expensive weekends, so we tried an anchorage in Pelican Bay where we were surrounded by mangroves, sandy beaches, aqua waters, and dolphins jumping through our wake. It was a beautiful sight until the wind kicked up. The boat was swinging back and forth on the anchor, causing it to dig deeper and deeper into the sand. By morning, the power wench could not lift the anchor. Clark started his two diesel engines and put the throttle in reverse to release it.

No, we didn't need that boat, but Clark got it free and clear in his divorce settlement. His wife wanted the house, so he got the boat. Clark had to laugh all the way to the bank because the boat was paid for but the house had a mortgage. Still, the dockage fees, insurance, diesel, and repairs were costly. We had the boat for sale for seven years before we got a reasonable offer from a private jet pilot who wanted it as his home address.

Then we said no more boats until Clark happened upon his former diesel mechanic, who was selling a twenty-five-foot 1998 Bayliner. The hull was in perfect condition with a high gloss shine and was cradled on a tandem trailer. The mechanic had rebuilt the engine and had replaced the fuel system and the gas tank. All that for only $5,000. Clark was so excited he rushed home to get me to look at the boat.

I agreed that the exterior was perfect for an older craft. We asked to see the cockpit and the cabin. The captain and mate chairs were brand new. The cabin's v-berth and bench-chair fabric were moldy and torn and had lost their color. The curtains were ripped from rot and mold. The dining table needed to be refinished, and the bathroom floor was broken-up sheet vinyl.

The ceiling and walls were covered with moldy, rusty carpet. I ran up two steps to the cockpit and yelled to Clark, "I love it!"

By now you know why. Clark and I could bleach the carpeted ceiling and walls, reupholster the chairs and bed, sew new curtains, refinish the table and countertops, tile the bathroom floor, and enjoy. Later, we discovered we didn't use the boat much, so we sold it at a tremendous profit.

Our next boat ride was courtesy of someone else—Royal Caribbean. The captain took us on our first cruise to the Caribbean, but it wasn't a very peaceful one. We left Florida in gale-force winds and high waves. The crew promised conditions would be calm in the Caribbean Sea. Not so! The waves were so high that we could not be tendered to the shores of the Grand Cayman Islands.

On our return trip across the Atlantic we were rolling around in our bed. I better clarify that. The rolling wave action was responsible. Taking a peek out of our balcony slider, we saw wave spray up to the ninth floor. No more boats!

CHAPTER 31

Miracles Happen If You
Believe in Them

God brought Clark to earth on February 18, 1947, and took Alex back to heaven on February 18, 2006. Why did He create and take a life on this same February day? That was not a coincidence but God's plan for our lives. During all those unhappy years, I never gave up. I waited for a change in my life. When I suffered, I wondered why, but I had to be patient and trust that God loved me. In time, maybe not my time schedule but His, the reasons for suffering became clear to me. The more I trusted God, the less I worried, and the less I worried the healthier I became.

Insurance companies consider annual physicals preventive medicine for people over sixty-five. To be on the safe side, we get annual exams to receive our benefits and to remain healthy as long as possible.

For four years, the doctor had checked my cerotic arteries and each time prescribed an ultrasound due to assumed blockage. Last year, he prescribed a CAT scan after the ultrasound. The following morning the doctor called my home and got right to the point. "You have a blood clot on your brain," he said. "Get to my office as quickly as possible. I have a bed waiting for you in the hospital next door."

I didn't know if I had time to take a shower, because he was waiting for me at his office. In hindsight, I realize that should not have been my top priority. From the doctor's office, I was taken by wheelchair directly into admissions. I was given hyperon intravenously to thin my blood. A neurosurgeon had already ordered a magnetic resonance angiography that took pictures to check the blood vessels in the brain for a clot.

Four days later, I was discharged. The test results showed no blood clot on the brain. Did the radiologist err in his diagnosis? The surgeon did find that one of the two sinus arteries in the back of my neck was deformed and useless. My right sinus artery was doing all the work. He said this was nothing to worry about since I'd probably had the problem since birth.

I wasn't about to accept my alarming diagnosis without a second opinion. On the Internet, I located a neurosurgeon in Sarasota, Florida, who had been educated at Harvard. After reading my films he said I had been hoodwinked by a radiologist not qualified to be in his profession. However, the doctor said he could diagnose problems only from the neck up and advised me to see a vascular surgeon about the potential cerotic artery blockage. He recommended the Sarasota Vascular Association.

The surgeon there did an examination and congratulated me for my clear cerotic arteries. There was no blockage and never had been. "What your primary doctor was hearing was a heart murmur, not a blockage," he said. Now I recalled how my gynecologist had diagnosed a heart murmur and would not prescribe birth control pills because of it. I was also instructed not to gain weight, which could make pregnancies problematic. The heart murmur has been a factor from one end of my life to another.

The neurosurgeon said arthritis was my greatest health concern. He could see my difficulty walking. I told him that I had had a series of X-rays on my lower back, hips, and shoulder and that an osteopathic surgeon would love to see me walk in his door and leave with two artificial hips, a new left shoulder, and a reconstructed back. The neurosurgeon recommended I go to the Sarasota Rheumatoid Arthritis Research Center for analysis. The bad news was that my arthritis was global, everywhere. Surgery was out of the question since I would be in surgery for the rest of my life. The good news was that the doctor had medication for me to try. To me that was bad news. A girlfriend had died at thirty-eight after arthritis medications caused a bleeding stomach. To the doctor's dismay, I declined the medication and chose to take Aleve occasionally.

I have seen many miracles in my lifetime. I believe that God intervenes in human affairs to stir people's awe and wonder, bearing witness to Himself. Was this another miracle? Did the blood clot disappear from one analysis to another? Was it never really there? Only God knows for sure. I put my life in His hands. He had a plan for me.

This next miracle may be more obvious. I was helping my elderly neighbor maintain her flower garden. Her hose would not reach the flower bed, so I filled a watering can at my outdoor faucet and walked back and forth down a grassy path from my house to hers. As I went for a last bucket, a bird flew down to snatch a three-foot black snake from the path I was about to enter. The bird dropped the snake in a patch of palmetto palms a few feet away. I am deathly afraid of snakes, and God is always taking care of me.

Here's another miracle. Clark's left arm was losing feeling and turning black. His general physician recommended a visit to the hospital. Clark was immediately put in intensive care. His breast muscle was cutting off all circulation to his arm. He was rushed to surgery to have a stent put in a vein to open the blood flow. Miraculously, before Clark went into surgery, his body produced new veins to provide blood to the arm. To this day, his upper arm has veins that only a superior being could create. Normally, arm veins are straight lines flowing up and down the arm. Clark's new veins formed a heart shape in his upper arm. Imagine that!

CHAPTER 32

The Smaller Our Needs Get,
the Bigger God Becomes

I became a member of the Bradenton Presbyterian Church
around 2003 when I needed to know what to do with my life.
I had lost everyone I brought with me to Florida. Ernest and Alex
had died needless deaths, and BSS's departure, though a blessing,
was nonetheless tragic. Because of his youth and the suddenness of
his death, Alex's funeral service may have been the most mournful
event ever experienced at the church. A few months later Ernest's
accident happened just a few yards from the church's front door.

Sitting in church alone made me feel isolated, so I joined the
choir. The members took me under their wing even if I wasn't
the most melodic bird in the cage. In conversations with them, I
explained why I was divorced and said that after losing most of my
family through deaths, I was now alone. I became the recipient
of prayer. Instead of shunning me, the folks in the choir cared for
me and still do.

My interests at church expanded to many more areas where
I felt I could help others through my experiences. When the
church offered a DivorceCare seminar to the general community,
I shared my Christian advice with people suffering through the
divorce process.

On Wednesday mornings, I became an office angel—a cute

term for a receptionist who greets people entering the church office area and answers calls coming into the church. Once a month on Thursdays, I packaged the monthly mailing to all the parishioners. I was replaced by the computer email service, but I soon found a church commitment that changed my life.

While I was still looking for a way to use my past and present experiences to help at church, I heard about the Stephens Ministry, a program designed to help suffering people. The church was asking for volunteers to head up the program and for caregivers to help those in need. A Stephens Ministry leader called me after the pastor suggested I would be a helpful listener for people suffering through divorce, loss of a job or a loved one, illness, depression, or loneliness.

She said the program's leaders received seventy hours of training and caregivers got fifty-two. She invited me to be a caregiver. I would be asked to learn what the care receiver was thinking, feeling, believing, and experiencing. In fervent prayer, we would depend on God to be the cure giver. Confidential meetings between the giver and the receiver would build trust. The one-hour meetings would take place every week in person, on the phone, or by email. About twenty caregivers would share their joys and burdens as they grew, changed, and were challenged on this journey.

The leader asked me to join in this caring relationship to share my unique combination of gifts, personality, and character. I gave her invitation prayerful thought and accepted the position. After four years as a caregiver, I feel more like a care receiver because of the good feeling I have knowing I have made someone else's life better. I have progressed in the ministry to become a facilitator who assists five other caregivers in their giving skills. God's plan has become a reality!

Clark has quite a different story about his journey with God, but we both ended up at the same place, in church. As a baby,

Clark was baptized in his father's Lutheran faith although his dad never attended church. His mother was a Catholic but also did not attend church. Clark was taught at home to love God and to be kind to others.

Because he was a state trooper, Clark's work schedule did not permit him to attend church on Sunday. It's too bad Sunday was the only day to worship back then. Fortunately, many churches now have Saturday evening and weekday services.

One Sunday morning, Clark drove by a Baptist church and saw the minister walking out to the parking lot. He stopped to say hello. The minister asked if he had been saved. The answer was no. The minister asked him if it would be okay if he prayed for his salvation right there in the parking lot. Clark accepted the blessing. After that, Clark would occasionally go to church with a friend. It wasn't until he found God in a little country church by the cottage and married me there that he started to attend church regularly.

When we were back in Florida we attended Bradenton Presbyterian Church. Clark was mesmerized by the pastor's sermons, which he felt were directed at him. He needed to hear more and became anxious to attend church every Sunday. It wasn't long before we were asked to collect the offering at the 9:40 a.m. service. Soon after, Clark was asked to be an elder of Christian education. A big job! Under his umbrella are Faithworks adult Bible study, men's and women's weekly Bible study, the Deep Blue children's Sunday school, and the youth group.

The head pastor also asked Clark to be on the nominating committee to elect deacons and elders and to be on the personnel committee, which is responsible for church staffing and evaluations. Being in charge of the youth group and serving on the personnel committee could have presented a conflict of interest when the youth group coordinator had to be replaced.

Clark not only had to recommend replacing the coordinator but had to do part of that job for the time being.

His first challenge was Lighthouse, a community project. On the fourth Sunday of the month, the youth group would prepare a meatloaf meal for 150 homeless people in Manatee County. With the help of a dozen teenagers and Pastor Chris, Clark and I made forty pounds of meatloaf, two gallons of gravy with mashed potatoes and beans, eight bags of tossed salad, and brownies. We were ready to get in the van, with just one stop at Dunkin' Donuts for refreshments before heading to the homeless shelter.

The teens love to participate in this ministry. It's a chance for them to bond in Christian love and to give to those in need. In my heart, I was apprehensive. I had never seen homeless people. Before I volunteered to participate with the youth group, I had heard that the homeless lived in the woods, most in tents. I wondered about their lifestyle. With no running water, how could they wash themselves or their clothes? They would have no toilets. What about refrigeration of food? For that matter, where could they get a daily meal?

I later learned that the Jesus Loves You Shelter offered overnight beds, showers, haircuts, clean clothes, and a food pantry. Until recently, the shelter had helped mostly men with only a handful of women in a small separate room. Now the number of women and children far surpassed the number of men.

At 5:00 p.m. the doors opened and I was pleasantly surprised to see smiling people with thankful hearts entering the shelter. Not all of them lived in the woods, but they definitely needed our loving support. Some lived in trailers and shacks and had few possessions. Hearing their comments, I realized they saw a difference between us. I wanted to reach out to them and tell them we were the same. No matter what our lifestyle, we are all God's children and have hardships, joys, and sorrows.

CHAPTER 33

Never Give Up

I'm finishing this story as Clark and I travel on the shores of the Gulf of Mexico. My years with Clark have been well worth the wait. I never gave up. I trusted God would get me through the hard times. If that was not His plan, I trusted I would spend eternal life in His home. Either way, I would win. I count every day with Clark as a gift from God. We are taking this trip inch by inch, stopping for anything we want to see or do. We're in no hurry to get home.

I wake up at 7:00 a.m. The sun is just peeking through the windows, and the mockingbirds are singing everybody else's song. I see my sweetheart, the love of my life, lying beside me. I listen to him breathe and feel his heart beat. I check his pulse, hoping to discover a normal beat. It is possible that his atrial fibrillation may disappear, but for now, he takes blood thinners to stop blood clots from traveling to his brain. Several years ago, Clark had two stents put in his heart arteries to open up the blood passage. He has since been pain-free.

We don't get up until we have to, because morning is the best time of the day to hold each other. Best of all, when Clark's eyes open and he sees me, a big smile lights up his face. That tells me everything! He doesn't have to say "I love you." I see it in his eyes.

We thank God every day for getting us up on the right side of the grass. At our age, we joke about never buying green bananas or filling the gas tank too high. We are aging and don't want to admit it. The other day, I realized the extent of Clark's hearing loss. We were listening to a TV game show when a contestant said he was a physical therapist. What Clark heard was that he was homeless and just out of the military.

A few days later Clark found himself at the audiologist's office partially hearing that he has a 70 percent hearing loss in one ear and a 20 percent loss in the other and needs a hearing aid, which he refuses to wear. I have learned to stand very close when I talk to him. That's no problem! I'm happy to be on his arm.

From my experiences, I know tomorrow may never come, so I hug and kiss Clark when he goes out the door to the store, and I wave and blow him a kiss as he drives away. I take the time to sit and talk about our previous day and about our dreams for tomorrow. But if tomorrow never comes I would thank God for giving us nine happy years together. I would cherish the memories and ponder them in my heart.

Many people ask me why God stood by and watched me struggle. God has now revealed Himself to me. I would not be writing this book if it were not for my past misfortunes. God is using me to tell His story of wondrous love for you and me. My journey with God has increased my faith that the Holy Spirit is in my heart. Faith in my heart is the assurance of things not seen. I can't see the future, but I know that Jesus is walking beside me and that I have nothing to fear.

When all is said and done, what really matters is loving the Lord God with all my heart, with all my soul, and with all my mind. Do I? Though I have an intense love for Clark, I am sure I love God more. That's because He gave me Clark. I wouldn't have him without God's plan. My heart overflows with love for

Clark. There is nothing he could do to make me love him more, and there is nothing he could do to make me love him less.

Next, God asks us to love our neighbors as ourselves. That sounds like a pretty big job, especially in the me-me culture of the twenty-first century. Just remember that joys and sorrows are shared by all. We're all the same, and we should treat each other with mutual respect. God asks us all to follow the Golden Rule and above all to believe in Jesus Christ as our Savior. If we do that, we will go to heaven.

Don Moen and Claire Cloninger wrote a song called "I Offer My Life," and I would like to share a few lines with you. The song seems to have been written for me, but the words tell about all of our lives.

I Offer My Life
Lord, I offer my life to You.
Everything I've been through, use it for Your glory.
Lord, I offer my days to You,
Lifting my praise to You as a pleasing sacrifice.

All that I am, all that I have,
I lay them down before You, O Lord,
All my regrets, all my acclaims,
The joy and the pains. I'm making them Yours.